D1048822

"Rumiko Takahashi's Maison Ikkoku is a fine achievement in comics storytelling. If you think this sounds like the stuff soap operas are made of, then you're right! And like the best soap operas, Maison Ikkoku is engaging, entertaining, and addictive."

Amazon.com

"This is really a heartwarming romantic comedy. At times it's just dropdead funny, other times it's truly romantic. It manages to maintain a good balance of both."

A Parent's Guide to Anime

"Maison Ikkoku has become a favorite with its touch of comedy and drama. The "relationship" between manager Kyoko and Godai is not only the source of many a laugh, but also one that is easily identifiable (though the story is uniquely Japanese)."

Official U.S. PlayStation Magazine

"Maison Ikkoku is an institution... There really is chemistry that comes through in the manga pages."

Anime News Network

"Maison Ikkoku is screwball romantic comedy at its finest."

Tony's Online Tips

VIZ GRAPHIC NOVEL

MAISON IKKOKU™ VOLUME NINE

LEARNING CURVES

STORY AND ART BY

RUMIKO TAKAHASHI

CONTENTS

This volume contains MAISON IKKOKU PART SIX #6 (second half) through #11 in their entirety.

STORY AND ART BY
RUMIKO TAKAHASHI

ENGLISH ADAPTATION BY
GERARD JONES

Translation/Mari Morimoto
Touch-Up Art & Lettering/Bill Spicer
Cover Design/Hidemi Sahara
Editor/Trish Ledoux
Assistant Editor/Annette Roman

Managing Editor/Hyoe Narita
Director of Sales & Marketing/Oliver Chin
Editor-in-Chief/Satoru Fujii
Publisher/Seiji Horibuchi

Printed in Canada

Published by Viz Communications, Inc.
P.O. Box 77010 • San Francisco, CA 94107

10 9 8 7 6 5 4 3 2
First Printing, January 1998

MAISON IKKOKU GRAPHIC NOVELS TO DATE

MAISON IKKOKU
FAMILY AFFAIRS
HOME SWEET HOME
GOOD HOUSEKEEPING
EMPTY NEST
BEDSIDE MANNERS
INTENSIVE CARE
DOMESTIC DISPUTE
LEARNING CURVES
DOGGED PURSUIT
STUDENT AFFAIRS

PART 1

INSTRUCTIONS FOR THE GUIDANCE AND SUPERVISION OF THE ANNUAL SPORTS FESTIVAL

WAK
WAK
PREPARATIONS FOR THE SPORTS FESTIVAL ARE IN FULL SWING.
AGAIN! AND LOUD THIS TIME, FROSHES!!
GO TEAM GO!

SUPERVISING THE PREPARATIONS WAS ALSO PART OF OUR STUDENT-TEACHER DUTIES. BUT THIS PART OF OUR JOB WAS VERY...
...VERY...
...VERY...
...ENJOY-ABLE !!
HI, MR. GODAI !
LUCKY GUY, TO HAVE SUCH A CUTE GIRL CHASING AFTER YOU.
NOT AS LUCKY AS YOU MIGHT THINK, BELIEVE ME.

THAT WIMPY GUY... HOW TYPICAL.
HMPH... BEING MANIPU-LATED BY A HIGH-SCHOOL STUDENT.
WELL, ANYWAY, WHEN THE SPORTS FESTIVAL IS OVER...
...THAT'S IT FOR THE STUDENT TEACHERS, TOO.
"GAME OVER," SO TO SPEAK.
THE SPORTS FESTIVAL, HUH...
?
WOW... BRINGS BACK MEMOR-IES...

GETTING TO INTERACT WITH STUDENTS OTHER THAN THOSE YOU TEACH--

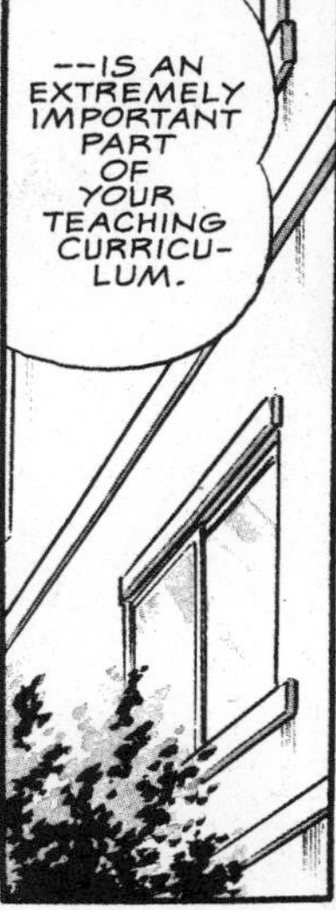
--IS AN EXTREMELY IMPORTANT PART OF YOUR TEACHING CURRICULUM.

THEREFORE, I WOULD LIKE ALL OF YOU STUDENT TEACHERS TO PROACTIVELY PARTICIPATE--
--IN ASSISTING WITH THE GUIDANCE AND SUPERVISION ASPECTS OF THE SPORTS FESTIVAL.
Freshmen | Sophomores

TO ENSURE EFFICIENCY, ANY DAY-TO-DAY COMMUNICATIONS AND DISCUSSIONS SHOULD BE HANDLED THROUGH EACH CLASS REPRESENTATIVE...
"CLASS REPRESENTATIVE"... ?

I'M CLASS REPRESENTATIVE.
OH, *GREAT.*

BY THE WAY...
YES?

IT SEEMS YOUR CLASS REPRESENTATIVE, IBUKI YAGAMI, HAS TAKEN QUITE A LIKING TO YOU...
WELL, YEAH, I GUESS.

SHE MAY BE A GROWN-UP IN BODY, BUT PLEASE REMEMBER THAT YOU'RE STILL DEALING WITH A CHILD.
YES, MA'AM.
DO NOT ALLOW YOURSELF TO GET CARRIED AWAY BY UNCONTROLLABLE LUST, I IMPLORE YOU.
AW, MA'AM! OF COURSE NOT!!
GEEZ, SHE SHOULDN'T BE WARNING ME!
I'M THE ONE WHO'S PRAYING THAT YAGAMI DOESN'T GET CARRIED AWAY!
LOCKER ROOM
HEY, YAGAMI! SO, LIKE, WHAT'S BEEN HAPPENING BETWEEN YOU AND MR. GODAI?
NOTHIN', ZILCH, NADA.
SO WHATCHA GONNA DO? HE'S GONNA BE GONE AFTER THE SPORTS FESTIVAL, Y'KNOW!
NO PROB-LEM!
I'M CLASS REPRESENTA-TIVE, REMEMBER?
HE'S GOTTA GO THROUGH ME FOR ALL THE SPORTS FESTIVAL STUFF.
SO THERE'S GONNA BE PLENTY OF CHANCES FOR ME TO BE ALONE WITH HIM, RIGHT?!

SEE YA!
DON'T FORGET, WE HAVE A MEETING OF THE HEAD CHEERLEADERS TOMORROW AT 7 A.M. SHARP!

2-4
'KAY, MR. GODAI...
...YOU'LL NEED TO COORDINATE THE FOLLOWING ITEMS...

SEE YA LATER, "CLASS REPRESENTATIVE"...!
YOU CAN DO IT, CLASS REPRESENTATIVE! HEE HEE HEEEE!

SO, UH, FROM HERE TO THE BACK OF THE BLEACHERS, IF YOU COULD...

MR. GODAI!
PLEASE LOOK AT THE DIAGRAM!
YEAH, SORRY.

OKAY... THE PERSON IN CHARGE WILL BE STANDING HERE...

I KNOW WHAT'S UP.

SHE'S HIT-TING ON ME.

UM... I THINK. NO, I'M SURE OF IT...

GEEZ, WHAT A KID.
SHE'S GOTTA BE KIDDING IF SHE THINKS THIS SORT OF THING CAN HAVE AN EFFECT ON ME. I MEAN, I'VE RESISTED AN OLDER, EXPERIENCED WOMAN LIKE KYOKO...
OH, TEACH...
U UP!!

SHRAA KKATA

OH... YOU'RE STILL HERE?

AND WHAT EXACTLY ARE YOU TWO DOING?
DISCUSSING THE SPORTS FESTIVAL, MA'AM. I AM THE CLASS REPRESENTATIVE, AFTER ALL!

I SEE.
I WOULD SUGGEST YOU WRAP THINGS UP AS SOON AS POS-SIBLE.
YES, MA'AM. WE'RE PRETTY MUCH DONE ALREADY, ANY-WAY.

IF SOMETHING HAPPENS, YOU WILL BE HELD PERSONALLY RESPONSIBLE.
I KNOW, I KNOW!

MR. GODAI !!
MAN, WHAT A PEST !

GEEZ, MR. GODAI !
YOU DON'T GOTTA RUN AWAY FROM ME!
OH, YEAH? SO... WHAT DO YOU WANT ?!

HERE, THIS NOTE-BOOK'S FOR YOU.
I WROTE DOWN ALL THE PLANS SO FAR IN IT.
I NEED YOU TO CHECK IT OVER BY TO-MORROW.

'KAY, SEE YA TO-MORROW !
SURE... SEE YOU.

THAT WAS DOWN-RIGHT SCARY.
GIRLS THESE DAYS... WHEW-WWW !!

BOY... HE'S GOT NO SELF-CONFI-DENCE AT ALL!
PISSES ME OFF !

I'M BACK!

WEL-COME HOME, GODAI.
YOU'RE KIND OF LATE TODAY.
YEAH.
PREPAR-ATIONS FOR THE SPORTS FESTI-VAL... STUFF LIKE THAT.
PIYO PIYO

.....

SO... HOW HAS IT BEEN GOING?
YOU KNOW... WITH THAT GIRL, IBUKI YAGAMI...?
EH-- ?!?

WH- WHY DO YOU ASK... ?!?
OH, JUST CURIOUS.

IT'S JUST THAT... WELL, GIRLS OF THAT AGE CAN BE SO TOTALLY FEARLESS.
SO I WAS WONDER-ING HOW YOU WERE DOING.

GIVE ME A BREAK!
SHE'S JUST A KID!
I-- I'M...
PIYO

...I'M ONLY ATTRACTED TO OLDER WOMEN.

PIYO

OH... REALLY. I-I SEE.
I... I DIDN'T MEAN--
THAT'S OKAY... JUST SO LONG AS WE UNDERSTAND EACH OTHER.

WHOA... WHAT A REACTION!
MAYBE SOMETHING DID HAPPEN...

CHI-RI-RI-RI

SNNN NFFF
PERFUME ??
NOW WHY...
...WOULD THAT BE ON A SPORTS FESTIVAL PLAN NOTEBOOK...?!

FLIP
NOTEBOOK
SPORTS FESTIVAL PLAN

.....!!
I LOVE YOU
I LOVE YOU
I LOVE YOU

FLIP
I LOVE YOU
I LOVE YOU

FLIP
I LOVE YOU
I LOVE YOU

FLIP FLIP FLIP
I LOVE YOU
I LOVE YOU
I LOVE YOU

WH-WHAT KIND OF A GUY DOES SHE THINK I AM!? A KID LIKE HER?!

OKAY. THIS TIME...
...I'VE REALLY GOT TO GIVE HER A GOOD CHEWING OUT!

SHE PROBABLY THINKS I'M A WUSS...
...THAT I'D NEVER YELL AT HER.

BUT EVEN I GET REALLY ANGRY SOMETIMES! AND I AM NOT...
...REPEAT, NOT GOING TO STAND FOR BEING PUSHED AROUND BY SOME BRATTY LITTLE HIGH-SCHOOL GIRL WITH A CRUSH!

HYAH!!
NO MORE !!

I'M GOING TO SCHOOL !!
UH... SEE YOU LATER.

BOY... WHAT WAS THAT ALL ABOUT ?
HMM ?
SNURF SNFF
OH, THAT'S RIGHT. POOR SOICHIRO... I HAVEN'T FED YOU YET, HAVE I.
OH, DEAR!
GODAI FORGOT TO TAKE THIS WITH HIM!
PIYO PIYO
TMP TMP
I'LL NEVER CATCH UP WITH HIM...
ESPECI-ALLY THE WAY HE TOOK OFF RUNNING TODAY !
"SPORTS FESTIVAL PLAN"... ??
HONESTLY, GODAI! FORGETTING SUCH AN IMPOR-TANT--
......
...
FLIP
I LOVE YOU
I LOVE YOU

OKAY, CLASS-- TODAY YOU WILL HAVE ONLY HALF A DAY OF CLASSES.
IN THE AFTERNOON, WE WILL BE DOING THE FINAL DRESS-REHEARSAL FOR THE SPORTS FESTIVAL.

NOW, THE ADMINISTRATION HAS GIVEN SEVERAL CAUTIONARY NOTICES...

SOME-HOW I'VE GOT TO GET HIM ALONE...
...AND TAKE THE NEXT STEP!

I GUESS I JUST CAN'T YELL AT HER IN FRONT OF THE WHOLE CLASS.
SOMEHOW I'VE GOT TO GET HER ALONE...

HE'S STARING AT ME...
I GUESS HE'S SEEN WHAT I WROTE IN THE NOTE-BOOK!

TEEE HEEE

CHUG CHUG CHUG

WHAT SHOULD I DO? IT'S NOT ANYTHING IMPORTANT ENOUGH TO DELIVER TO HIM, IS IT...?

BUT...

MY OLD HIGH SCHOOL, HMM?

AT MY AGE, IT'S HARD TO FIND AN EXCUSE TO VISIT ANY MORE...

WOW... NOTHING'S CHANGED AT ALL!
IT'S SO NOSTAL-GIC!

IT'S THE LANDLADY FROM MR. GODAI'S PLACE!
HEY!
CHECK IT OUT!

THAT OLD WIDOW'S HERE !?!

THAT PUSHY OLD BROAD! GEEZ !!
YEAH! AN'SHE'S HERE TO SEE MR. GODAI, I BET!
SMILE

ER... HI.

OH!
HELLO!
SO, UHH... WHAT'S UP... ?
HOW COME YOU CAME ALL THE WAY OUT HERE TO THE SCHOOL?

WELL, GODAI FORGOT THIS...
...SO I CAME HERE TO DELIVER IT.

HEY !!
TH-THAT'S MINE !!
OH, REALLY ?

GOOD. THAT SAVES ME THE TROUBLE OF HAVING TO LOOK FOR HIM.
SEE YOU!

THEY THINK I'M JUST A DUMB KID.
I MEAN, WHY WOULD THAT OL' LADY BRING THIS?!

JUST YOU WATCH !
NO MAN CAN RESIST A CUTE YOUNG GIRL LIKE ME!!

WHAT ?! ARE YOU NUTS ?!?
YAGAMI, YOU'VE FINALLY LOST IT!
DON'T SWEAT IT-- IT'S ONLY TO GET HIS FULL ATTEN-TION.
I HOPE I WON'T HAVE TO SAY "I TOLD YOU SO."
YEAH... YOU'RE IN FOR IT BIG TIME IF THE TEACHER FINDS OUT!

JUST GET HIM THERE AND SHUT UP, OKAY?!
YOU'RE TAKING ALL THE BLAME IF SOMETHING HAPPENS, ALL RIGHT?!

HAVE YOU SEEN IBUKI YAGAMI ?
NOPE.

YEESH... I TRY TO GET HER ALONE...
...AND SHE DIS-APPEARS ON ME !

HEY! THERE HE IS!
MR. GODAI !

YOU GOTTA COME WITH US, OKAY ?!

GYM STORAGE

THERE WAS SOME KINDA WEIRD SOUND COMING FROM IN THERE!
ORAGE

WHOOD

WHA-- ?!
SLAM

HEY !!
THD THD
OPEN UP !

Ohhhh... TEACH...
ULP!

YAGAMI !?!
WH-WHAT THE HELL DO YOU THINK YOU'RE DOING?! PUT YOUR CLOTHES BACK--
LOWER YOUR VOICE!

IF YOU DON'T DO EXACTLY WHAT I SAY, I'M GOING TO SCREAM!

....

IT REALLY IS NOSTAL-GIC!
YOU'VE REALLY GROWN UP, MISS CHIGUSA.
FACULTY

OH, I MEAN, MRS. OTONASHI.
I'M SORRY-- OLD HABITS DIE HARD.
I REMEMBER ALWAYS BEING SCOLDED BY YOU...

SAY... THAT STUDENT TEACHER, YUSAKU GODAI... DOESN'T HE LIVE IN YOUR APARTMENT HOUSE?
YES... HOW IS HE DOING?

WELL, HE'S GETTING PUSHED AROUND A BIT BY THIS ONE GROUP OF STUDENTS, BUT...
OH, YES... SO I HEARD.

WILL YOU CUT IT OUT AL-READY ?!?
WE'RE GOING TO BE IN DEEP TROUBLE IF WE GET CAUGHT LIKE THIS!
WHAT DO YOU MEAN "WE"... ?!?
THUNK
THAK

HONEST, I SWEAR I'M NOT DOING THIS TO GET YOU INTO TROUBLE, MR. GODAI...
YOU'RE DOING IT ANY-WAY!
TUMP
TUMP

DAMMIT, YAGAMI! YOU SHOULD BE SAVING YOURSELF FOR MARRIAGE!
P.U.! WHAT A STINKY LINE!
HEY, THAT REMINDS ME... DID YOU GUYS WATCH THAT MOVIE OF THE WEEK LAST NIGHT?
IT WAS A RE-RUN, BUT...

WHY DON'T YOU COME TO THE SPORTS FESTI-VAL?
YES... MAYBE I WILL!

HM?
THUNK

GOOD HEAVENS... ARE THERE STILL STUDENTS AROUND?
THEY SHOULD HAVE GONE HOME BY NOW...

≡SIGH≡ ...ALL THE STUDENTS GET SO WORKED UP WHEN THERE'S A SPECIAL EVENT APPROACHING...
THAK

IF YOU DON'T STOP THIS RIGHT NOW, IBUKI YAGAMI, I'M REALLY GOING TO GET REALLY, REALLY ANGRY!!
.......!
KUCH...

G-G-GODAI...!?!

WHAT? WHAT?! YOU THINK I'M UGLY OR SOMETHING?!

I-I... D-DON'T BE RIDICU-LOUS!!
AND WHAT IS THAT SUP-POSED TO MEAN?

IT'S EXACTLY THAT SORT OF WISHY-WASHY BEHAVIOR THAT LETS THEM TAKE ADVANTAGE OF YOU!
SHOW A LITTLE SPINE FOR A CHANGE!

THAT OLD WIDOW LADY, RIGHT?!?
I LOVE SOME-ONE ELSE, YAGAMI!!

....
!

....

DON'T LIE TO ME
!
TH-THAT'S NONE OF YOUR--

W-W-WAIT... I DIDN'T TELL YOU--
THAT'S IT. I'M GETTING OUT...
!!

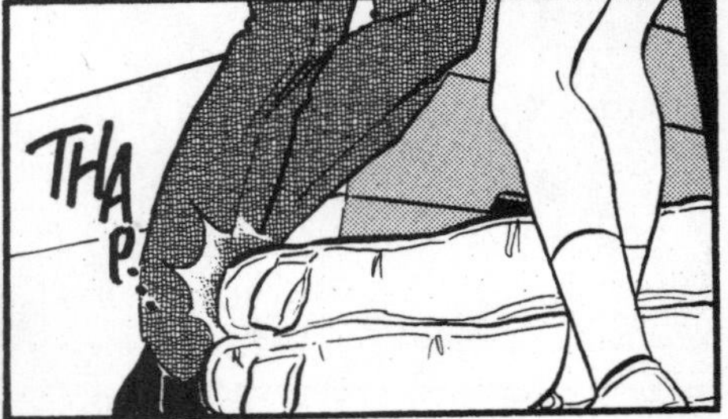
THAP

EEEEK!
FWUD...

I NEVER PLANNED TO... I MEAN, I DIDN'T THINK WE'D...
N-N-NOW WHAT DO I DO--?
B-BUT NOW MAYBE I HAVE TO...

K-K...
KYOKO ?!?
WHAM
MISS YAGAMI, WOULD YOU PLEASE COME WITH ME TO THE PRINCIPAL'S OFFICE?
ALL RIGHT, THAT'S ENOUGH !!
EEK?

EXCUSE ME, MA'AM, BUT HOW FAR ARE YOU GOING TO LET THIS GO?
OH, SORRY. I JUST GOT KIND OF MES-MER-IZED...

I TOLD YOU SO, YAGAMI!!
GEEZ.
...AND YOU MAY FIND YOURSELF IN A VERY SERIOUS SITUATION!
...THE MAN MAY SUDDENLY DECIDE YOU MEAN IT...
YOU MAY THINK OF IT AS INNOCENT TEASING, BUT...
YADDA YADDA YADDA

THANK GOD...
...THANK GOD I DIDN'T LOSE CONTROL!

I MEAN, THAT THEY DIDN'T CHARGE YOU.
AREN'T YOU GLAD?
OF COURSE!

...IS EVEN GOING TO SLOW ME DOWN!!
HMPH... AS IF THIS LITTLE BIT OF TROUBLE...
YADDA YADDA YADDA YADDA

PART 2

PAJAMA PARTY

DINNNNNGG
THE SPORTS FESTIVAL ENDED WITHOUT FURTHER ADO...
...AND, THE FOLLOWING SATURDAY...
...SO DID THE STUDENT-TEACHING PERIOD.
FINALLY. THE DAY AFTER TOMORROW... IT'S OVER.
I'VE NEVER BEEN SO STRES-SED!
AND SO...
OHH, MR. GODAI...
...IS THIS REALLY THE END FOR US?
"END," YAGAMI?
I THOUGHT YOU HAD HIM HOOKED.
SO DID I.
BUT THE FATES ARE AGAINST ME.
THAT'S ALL VERY NICE. BUT COULD SOMEBODY DO SOME CLEANING?!?

EVER SINCE...
...WELL, YOU KNOW... THE HOMEROOM TEACHER'S BEEN ON HER GUARD.

AND THAT WIDOW... SHE'S THE MAIN PROBLEM!

WE CAN'T BE SURE.
BUT RIGHT AFTER THE... UMM... GYM STORAGE ROOM INCIDENT...
AHA! SO IT'S TRUE!
MR. GODAI AND THAT LANDLADY OF HIS ARE AN ITEM!

HAPPILY!
COME ON, GODAI. LET'S GO HOME.
WELL, FROM A "BYSTANDER'S PERSPECTIVE"...
...IT DOES SEEM THAT HE WAS AMBUSHED.
GYM STORAGE
SO THEN, IS MR. GODAI OFF THE HOOK?

IT LOOKED LIKE...
HE WAS TAGGING AFTER HER LIKE A PUPPY.
NOT LIKE SHE'S JUST LOOKING OUT FOR HIM, BUT...
SOMETHING KINDA... WEIRDER...

RIGHT, YAGAMI?
STOP JUMPING TO CONCLUSIONS!

I MEAN, SHE'S SO OLD!
HOW COULD HE POSSIBLY WANT HER MORE THAN ME?

WAIT... THAT'S RIGHT. THE WIDOW DID SEEM KIND OF...

...CLOSE... TO THE HOMEROOM TEACHER.
AND IT'S LIKE SHE'D DEFINITELY BEEN TO THE SCHOOL BEFORE!

HMM.

I'LL SEE YOU LATER.
GOOD-BYE!

.....
....

MA'AM?
OH. YAGAMI.

WELL, HAVE YOU COME TO YOUR SENSES, YET?
OH PLEASE! ARE YOU STILL WORRYING ABOUT THAT?

DO YOU MEAN TO TELL ME YOU'RE NOT?
I'M NOT THE TYPE TO REMEMBER.

GOOD. THEN MAKE USE OF THAT PART OF YOUR PERSONALITY...
...BY FORGETTING ABOUT MR. GODAI HIMSELF.
THE STUDENT-TEACHING PERIOD IS ENDING ANYWAY, YOU KNOW.

UMM... BY THE WAY...

THAT SPINSTER...
I MEAN, WIDOW...
MEANING KYOKO OTONASHI, PERCHANCE...?

...EXCEPT SHE WASN'T HALF SO EXTREME.

....

SO!

THE BLACK WIDOW CAUGHT PREY OF HER OWN, DID SHE?

WHO IS *SHE* TO CRITICIZE WHAT I'M PLANNING...

...FOR "HER" PRECIOUS MR. GODAI ?!?

OKAY. TIME TO SETTLE THIS.

GOOD-BYE!
LATER!

YAGAMI...
GULP!
MR. GODAI!

DOING...? I DON'T REALLY... HAVE ANY...
WHAT ARE YOU DOING SUNDAY? TOMORROW, I MEAN!
HE'S FREAKIN' OUT!
WHO WOULDN'T?

UH...?
OKAY, THEN!
I'LL DROP BY YOUR BOARDING HOUSE AND PAY YOU A VISIT!

MY GRANDMA IS IN CRITICAL CONDITION, AND...
B-BUT THAT'S... I MEAN...
COME ON, MR. GODAI...

...DON'T BE SO JUMPY!
I MEAN, THESE GUYS ARE COMING WITH ME!
HUH... ???

YOU DON'T HAVE TO BE AFRAID OF ALL OF US, DO YOU?
WELL...IT'S NOT REALLY A MATTER OF BEING SCARED...
WE'RE WHAT--?
TOMORROW ?!?

THEN IT'S A DATE !
C'MON, MAKE ME A PINKIE-PROMISE !

SEE YOU TO-MOR-ROW !
THE SPORTS FESTIVAL ENDED WITHOUT FURTHER ADO...

...AND SO, THE FOLLOWING SATURDAY, DID THE STUDENT-TEACHING PERIOD...

TOOO-MORRR-ROW !!
...BUT SOME THINGS DON'T END SO EASILY.

WEL-COME HOME, GODAI!
SO, MONDAY'S YOUR LAST DAY, ISN'T IT?
OF STUDENT-TEACHING, I MEAN.
YEAH... WELL...
SIGH...
IT'S NOT OVER WHERE THE YAGAMI GIRL'S CONCERNED?
UH...
GULP!

I DON'T CARE WHAT SHE SAYS, I...
I... I... I... I... I...
OOPS! SORRY IF I UPSET YOU.

IT'S JUST THAT...
WELL, SHE KNOWS WHERE YOU LIVE, SO...
!!

THAT'S THE THING.
ONCE THEY KNOW YOUR ADDRESS AND PHONE NUMBER...
...THEY MAY AS WELL HAVE YOU IN A CAGE.
Chest

OKAY. TOMOR-ROW.
I'VE GOTTA MAKE IT CLEAR TO HER...

MMMM
SIGH SIGHH
MMMM
Chest

DO YOU GET IT NOW?!
I'M TAKEN!
OH, YEAH. DON'T I WISH.

LIKE KYOKO'S JUST GOING TO SIT THERE AND LET ME DROOL AND SIGH ALL OVER HER...
YOU BET.
WHAM
OH, GET REAL!

THERE'S NOTHING BETWEEN MR. GODAI AND I--!!
OH, COOL! THANK YOU!
...BAD, BAD, BAD.
SIGH.

SORRY TO IMPOSE!
C'MON IN.

TP TP TP
KLIK...

SORRY ABOUT LAST TIME.
OH...

.....
....
YEAH, SORRY.

HUH?
PSST, GODAI... C'MERE.

....
...
SOUNDS LIKE A COUPLE TO ME!
PSST PSST
I DIDN'T THINK YOU'D...
COULDN'T YOU AT LEAST HAVE TOLD ME ABOUT THIS?
I COULD HAVE PRE-PARED SOME-THING.

OH, DON'T WORRY ABOUT IT, MRS. OTONASHI!

I MEAN, MR. GODAI'S SINGLE, RIGHT? I FIGURED HE WOULDN'T HAVE ANYTHING...

...SO I BROUGHT GROCERIES!

WELL, WELL...

LET ME COOK LUNCH FOR YOU, MR. G.!

I...I GUESS.

UH... THANKS!

PIYO

AGGRES-SIVE LITTLE THING...

...BUT THEN, SHE'LL HARDLY BE OUT OF PLACE HERE.

EVENING CAME, WITH NO ADO...
GOO' BYE !
THANKS FOR HAVING US !

SEE YOU IN SCHOOL !
Chest
PIYO

Chest

YOU WANT TO SPEND THE NIGHT ?!?

NO NO NO NO NO NO NO NO NO NO NO NO NO NO NO!!

I CAN'T GO HOME !!
BUT, I ALREADY TOLD MY PARENTS I WAS SLEEPING OVER AT A FRIEND'S HOUSE!!

CAN'T !
YOU CAN !

I'LL THROW YOU OUT ON YOUR BUTT, IF I HAVE TO!
THEN DO IT! I DARE YOU!
WELL, IT'S FINALLY GETTING INTERESTING!

LISTEN, PEOPLE ARE ALREADY STARTING TO SAY THAT--
SAY WHAT? THAT YOU GRABBED A QUICK FEEL ON MY CHEST?

WHA... WHA... WHA...

IN THE GYM STORAGE ROOM, OR HAVE YOU FORGOTTEN!?
TH-TH-TH-TH--

HMM. SOUNDS SERIOUS...

--THAT WAS AN ACCIDENT!!
YOU'RE THE ONE WHO AMBUSHED ME!
WAS IT NOW?

'COURSE, KNOWING GODAI...
...HE PROBABLY GROPED HER CHEST ON PURPOSE AND MADE IT LOOK LIKE AN ACCIDENT.
....

BAM
WILL YOU *PLEASE* NOT ADD YOUR LOUSY TWO CENTS--

OH. H-HEY THERE, MANAGER.

UM...
PER-HAPS YOU SHOULD KEEP IT DOWN...

NO! I WON'T TOLERATE THIS IDIOCY!
TODAY I'LL END THIS ONCE AND FOR ALL!

LISTEN, KID...
EVEN FOR TEEN-AGERS, THERE ARE SOCIAL RULES THAT...
KLIKK

YOU... GRABBED... MY... CHEST...
H-HEY, WAIT A SECOND... THERE'S NOTHING TO...

WAA AAH!
NOW NO ONE WILL MARRY ME !!
YA-YA-YA-YAGAMI !!

BOOM
WHAT IS GOING ON IN HERE-- ?!?
PIYO PIYO

.....
....
Chest

AS I'M SURE YOU CAN SEE...

...I CAN'T GO HOME NOW !
.....
....

PART 3

PEEJAYS AND NEGLIGEES

THERE IS NO GREATER JOY THAN A CROWDED TABLE.
I AM MOST HONORED FOR HAVING BEEN INVITED.
YEAH, TOO BAD YOU WEREN'T!!
WHEN DO I GET TO EAT?!

YOU MUST LET HER STAY, GODAI.
YOU'VE GOT TO BE KIDDING!
chest

LISTEN, YAGAMI... YOU GO STRAIGHT HOME WHEN YOU'RE DONE EATING.
I'LL WALK YOU TO THE TRAIN.
I CAN'T GO HOME IN MY PAJAMAS!
Chest

YOU CAN CHANGE!
SORRY, NO CAN DO.

GOOD LORD.
WHAT IN THE WORLD IS THAT CHILD PLAN-NING?

WOULD SHE REALLY BE CONTENT JUST...
...SLEEP-ING IN GODAI'S ROOM?

WELL, GOOD NIGHT!
GOOD NIGHT!

GOOD MORNING-ING!
MORNING!
WHAT'S THE POINT?

CRIPES. I KNOW I'M NOT GONNA DO ANYTHING TO HER I'M NOT SUPPOSED TO...
...BUT THERE'S SUCH A THING AS PUBLIC OPINION!

OH, MAN! I *ATE!*
IT WAS EXQUISITE.
OKAY... *NOW*...
WHADDYA SAY, SHALL WE DO THE HONORS...?
WHY NOT?
ZHOOP
CLATTER
HUH??
MOVE.
HEY, WAIT, WHAT DO YOU THINK YOU'RE...

TAAAAAAADAAAA

DO YOU KNOW WHAT YOU'RE SAYING?!
PLEASE, SETTLE INTO THE BRIDAL BED. DO NOT LET OUR PRESENCE HINDER YOU.

EASY, BOY. YOU'RE DROOLING.
I'M SO SICK OF THESE SLEAZY JOKES THAT--
Chest

B-B-BUT...
COME ON, NOW, HONEY, JUST SLIP ON IN--
!!

W-WAIT! THIS IS TOO QUICK...
DON'T BE SILLY!
IT'S LATE... YOU'RE IN YOUR JAMMIES...
...WHAT ELSE WOULD YOU DO BUT SLEEP?
....
AHEM WELL...

THIS IS YOUR LAST CHANCE.
PIYO PIYO

THESE GOONS AREN'T AFRAID OF ANYTHING !!
IF YOU THINK THESE PEOPLE ARE ONLY JOKING, THINK AGAIN.
WA HA HA
Chest

....

LAUGHING AT ME... BECAUSE SHE THINKS I'M JUST A CHILD...
THAT LOOK...
PIYO PIYO

ZZIIPP

SHE'S A TOUGH ONE, ALL RIGHT...

OKAY. OKAY.

I GIVE UP. YOU CAN STAY.
!!

I'LL SPEND THE NIGHT IN YOTSUYA'S ROOM...
NO, THANK YOU.

....
CHIK

O-KAY. THEN I'LL STAY IN NIKAIDO'S--
SORRY!
I CAN'T SLEEP WITH OTHER PEOPLE AROUND!
BAM

WE'VE ALREADY GOT THREE STUFFED INTO OUR PLACE.
AND I DON'T WANT TO GET PREGNANT YET.
HEY !!

OH, ALL RIGHT.

YOU CAN SLEEP IN MY ROOM.
WHA--

B-B-BUT, KYOKO...
IT CAN'T BE HELPED.
SO *THAT'S* HOW SHE'S GOING TO HOOK HIM!

WIDOWS!
I GUESS SHE THINKS SHE CAN GET AWAY WITH ANYTHING!

B-BUT... UM... UH...
...ARE YOU SURE IT'S OKAY IF I...
WHAT ARE YOU TALKING ABOUT?
GASP!

COME ON, KIDDO. GET UP.
YOU'RE COMING WITH ME.
Chest
WHA--

OHHHHHH...

WHY DIDN'T SHE SAY SO IN THE FIRST PLACE?
VIPP

WELL, GOOD NIGHT, ALL.
SEE YOU TO-MORROW!
UH...
A LITTLE TOO CALM ABOUT IT, YEAH?

DON'T WORRY ABOUT IT.
SORRY TO CAUSE YOU SO MUCH TROUBLE!

THIS IS IT...
...IT'S THE PERFECT OPPORTUNITY TO PERSUADE HER TO STOP HOUNDING GODAI...

...AL-THOUGH, I MUST SAY...
...SHE HARDLY SEEMS LIKE THE TYPE TO BE "PERSUADED" OF ANYTHING.
Y'KNOW, YOU'RE LIKE A MENTOR TO ME.
I... WHAT?

I'VE BEEN MEANING TO TALK TO YOU, AS ONE STUDENT TO ANOTHER...
WAIT A MINUTE. "STUDENT"??

YOU *DID* GRADUATE FROM MY HIGH SCHOOL, DIDN'T YOU?
WELL... YES... BUT...
PIYO PIYO
WHAT ON EARTH IS SHE PULLING *NOW?*

TOUGH LUCK, KIDDO.
YOU'RE TOO WORRIED ABOUT "APPEARANCES." YOU SHOULDA JUST LET HER STAY.
ARE YOU INSANE ?!?

IT'S NOT LIKE YOU'RE IN A POSITION TO TAKE YOUR PICK.
A CUTE YOUNG CHICK THROWING HERSELF AT YOU LIKE THAT? TSK, TSK.
I DON'T FIND THIS FUNNY.

THIS WAS YOUR CHANCE TO GET HER OFF THE ROLLER COASTER!
WHY TAKE THAT UP-AND-DOWN WITH KYOKO WHEN YOU CAN HAVE A LOVE-SLAVE OF YOUR OWN?
OH, COME ON...
THAT LI'L GIRL'S GOT IT BAD.
NOT EVEN A TEENAGER WOULD GO THIS FAR JUST FOR A JOKE.
.....
....

NO... THERE'S NO WAY...
SHE CAN'T BE SERI-OUS.
HE'S BUYIN' IT--!
WHAT A SUCKER!
MUMBLE MUMBLE

SAY, SCHOOL-MATE?
YES?
WERE YOUR BREASTS THAT BIG WHEN YOU WERE IN HIGH SCHOOL?
....
NOW SHE'S CHECKING ME OUT LIKE I'M... LIKE I'M LIVESTOCK!
NO. IN FACT, THEY WERE ABOUT LIKE YOURS.
YOUR HUSBAND!
YOU MARRIED YOUR TEACHER, RIGHT?
Y-Y-YES...
COOL! THEN YOU SNAGGED HIM JUST BY BEING CUTE--?!
......?

TELL ME HOW YOU DID IT! BE MY MENTOR! BE MY TEACHER!
LET ME STUDY AT YOUR FEET!
.....
....

PARDON ME, BUT I HAVE TO ASK...

...DO YOU REALLY, SERIOUSLY, LIKE MR. GODAI ??
YES !

.....
....

YOU'RE TEASING HIM BECAUSE YOU'VE GOT NOTHING BETTER TO DO, IS THAT IT?
OH, PLEASE.
THEN... IT'S A PASSING FANCY ?
ABSO-LUTELY NOT !
WHAT DO YOU SEE IN HIM?

IS IT WRONG FOR ME TO LIKE MR. GODAI?

WELL, NO... IT'S NOT WRONG...
IT'S JUST... THE WAY YOU'VE BEHAVED.
YOU THINK I'M INSANE?

NO, BUT YOU ARE... A BIT UN-USUAL.
WHO CARES?

ALL I WANT TO HEAR IS HOW A STUDENT CAN WIN HER TEACHER'S HEART...
...STRAIGHT FROM THE MOUTH OF A WOMAN WHO TRIED...AND WON!

YOU HAVE SCHOOL TOMOR-ROW.
IT'S TIME TO SLEEP.
....

I CAN'T RELAX...
I KNOW YAGAMI'S NOT JUST GOING TO GO MEEKLY TO SLEEP...

DON'T TELL ME SHE'D... SHE'D...
HEH HEH HEHH...

GASP!

JUST TELL ME.
.....
.....
MANAGER

PLEASE!
.....
.....

DON'T PRETEND TO BE ASLEEP...

I KNOW YOU'RE REALLY IN LOVE WITH MR. GODAI, TOO!
FLIPP

I'M RIGHT, AREN'T I?
THAT'S WHY YOU'RE ALWAYS INTER-FERING!
WHEN DID I EVER INTERFERE WITH YOU?

YOU KEPT ME FROM STAYING IN HIS ROOM.
WHAT ARE YOU SAYING? I SAVED YOU!

I KNOW THIS WILL BE HARD TO BELIEVE, FROM THE WAY HE'S BEEN ACTING...

...BUT YOUR "MR. GODAI" CAN BE JUST AS MUCH AN ANIMAL AS ANY ADOLESCENT BOY!

IF YOU'D STAYED IN HIS ROOM, YOU'D HAVE GOTTEN FAR MORE THAN YOU'RE READY FOR!

....

WHAT THE--?! HERE I AM, ALL WORRIED ABOUT HER AND CHECKING TO MAKE SURE SHE'S OKAY...

...AND SHE'S CALLING ME AN "ANIMAL" !!

YOU HAVE TO TREAT YOURSELF WITH MORE RESPECT, CHILD!
WHAT A CHUMP I AM. I'M GOING BACK TO SLEEP.

EX-CUSE ME...?
LET'S DROP THE GENERALIZATIONS, SHALL WE?

IT'S MY JOB!
WHY DO YOU KEEP INTERFERING?

...I HAVE TO DEAL WITH MY TENANTS' QUARRELS AND--
AS BUILDING MANAGER...
DO YOU HAVE TO RUN THEIR LOVE LIVES, TOO ??

....

I DIDN'T WANT TO HAVE TO TELL HER THIS, BUT...
THERE'S NO OTHER WAY...

MISS YAGAMI.
I HAVE TO TELL YOU THE TRUTH.

YOU SEE, MR. GODAI...
...IS IN LOVE WITH ME.

AND...?
"AND"...??

AND WHAT ABOUT YOU?
UM... UH...
ME...?

I... WELL... NO.

YOU DON'T?! OH, THANK YOU!

THEN IT'S ALL ON HIS SIDE !
THAT'S PERFECT !!
......
......

SIGH
G'NIGHT !!

ZZZZ
ZZZZ...
......
......

WE'RE OFF!

HAVE A GOOD DAY !
PIYO PIYO

C'MON, LET'S HURRY!
WE'LL BE LATE!
DON'T THEY LOOK CUTE TOGETHER?
OH, VERY.
PIYO PIYO
KRRACK
HUH?
MY, MY.
......
......
THEY JUST DON'T MAKE BAMBOO LIKE THEY USED TO.
DO THEY?
PIYO PIYO

PART 4

THE LONG GOOD-BYE

G'MORNING!
MORNING!
HA HA HA
YA AA A
WHEE
UMM... COULD YOU LET GO OF MY ARM, PLEASE?
YOU'RE RIGHT. WE DON'T WANT TO ATTRACT ATTENTION, DO WE?
YAGAMI!
OH, 'MORNING!
"'MORNING"?? GIVE ME A BREAK. GET OVER HERE!

DON'T TELL ME.
YOU REALLY STAYED AT MR. GODAI'S LAST NIGHT?
YEAH. I TOLD YOU I WOULD.

....

YOU SLEPT WITH MR. GODAI?!!
WHAT WAS IT LIKE?! WHAT WAS IT LIKE?!
THAT DOES IT! THIS IS GETTING OUT OF HAND!!

YOU SHOULD HAVE THOUGHT OF THAT EARLIER.

UHH---
UH-OH. BOSS LADY!
GO! GO!

TO BEGIN WITH, WALKING ARM-IN-ARM, FIRST THING IN THE MORNING...

...SURELY YOU REALIZE THE EFFECT THAT MIGHT HAVE ON THE OTHER STUDENTS...

BLAH BLAH

I'M VERY SORRY.

I'VE SEEN PLENTY OF STUDENT-TEACHERS COME AND GO IN MY TIME...

...BUT I'VE NEVER HAD TO LECTURE ONE SO MANY TIMES...

SORRY.

...ON THE OTHER HAND, WHEN I REALIZE THAT TODAY IS THE LAST DAY I'LL BE ADMONISHING YOU, I FEEL A CERTAIN SADNESS...

THAT MAKES *ONE* OF US...

THE LAST DAY OF STUDENT-TEACHING...

ALL STUDENTS...

...PLEASE GATHER IN THE AUDITORIUM !

...AND SO... UHHH... WE...

...TODAY...WE... UMM...BID OUR STUDENT-TEACHERS... AHHH...

YADDA YADDA YADDA YADDA YADDA YADDA YADDA

...KNOWING YAGAMI...

...SHE'S PROBABLY GOING TO KEEP SHOWING UP AT MAISON IKKOKU...

WHOA, WHOA, WHOA...

...IN THE *WIDOW'S* ROOM ?!?

UH-HUH.

WHAT?! YAGAMI ?!?

PSST

YEAH! ALL NIGHT LONG! AND...

PSST PSST

PSST

SHE'S GOT GUTS...

HEY! WHERE *IS* YAGAMI?!

SHE'S CUT-TING!

WHAT A JOKE.
THEN IT WAS TOTALLY POINTLESS !!
NOT HARDLY.
I SETTLED SOME THINGS.

G-TUK G-TUK G-TUK
YOU SEE, MR. GODAI...
...HAS A CRUSH ON *ME*.
AND WHAT ABOUT YOU?
UM... ME...?
I... WELL... NO...
YOU DON'T?! OH, THANK YOU !!

THAT LITTLE...
THAT'S PER-FECT!
THEN IT'S ALL ON HIS SIDE!
MAYBE I SHOULD'VE JUST SAID "I LOVE HIM RIGHT BACK"...
OR... SOME-THING...
I GO OUT OF MY WAY TO CAUTION HER, AND SHE... SHE...
AAARRH!
G-TUK G-TUK
HOW DO YOU TALK A GIRL LIKE THAT OUT OF ANYTHING?
BUT THAT MIGHT'VE JUST FUELED HER OBSESSION.
G-TUK G-TUK

IF YOU'D MADE ANY HEADWAY AT ALL, YOU'D STILL HAVE A CHANCE, BUT...
NOW YOU'RE HARDLY EVER EVEN GONNA SEE HIM!

YOU ALWAYS LOSE INTEREST REALLY QUICK ANYWAY, YAGAMI.
DON'T MAKE FUN OF ME!
THIS IS A REALLY SERIOUS THING FOR ME!

DING-DONNNNGG
OH, SHOOT!
HOME-ROOM'S GONNA START!
LET'S GO!

THEY'VE GOT A POINT, THOUGH...
I'M NOT GONNA SEE HIM AT SCHOOL ANY MORE...

IT'S PROBABLY SAFEST JUST TO LEAVE HER ALONE UNTIL HER "FEVER" BREAKS.
GODAI'S STUDENT-TEACHING IS ALL OVER NOW, ANYWAY...

MY ONLY HOPE WILL BE TO TRAVEL ALL THE WAY TO HIS APARTMENT HOUSE.
IT'S GOING TO TAKE DEDICATION.
AM I REALLY UP FOR THIS...?

WHAT AM I SAYING? OF COURSE I AM!
I HAVE TO BE!

WE... UH...
...HAD TO GO TO THE BATHROOM!
YADDA YADDA YADDA
AND WHAT ARE YOU GIRLS UP TO?
HM.

SUFFERING ALL THIS... FOR MY SECRET LOVE...
I'M SO INSPIRING...

OOOOM
GASP

YADDA YADDA YADDA
EEP!

HWOOOOOOOOOOOOOOOOO?
MR. GODAI
YAGAMI
HAPPY ENGAGEMENT!

CONGRA-TULATIONS, YAGAMI!
WE HEARD EVERY-THING!
KLUNK

WHAT'S IT LIKE, THE FIRST TIME AND ALL?
FOR THE SCHOOL PAPER!
IS IT TRUE YOU AND MR. GODAI REALLY... Y'KNOW... Y'KNOW...??
KLUNK KLUNKK

WHAT?
....
IT'S A LIE!!

YOU'RE BEING SO... RUDE!!
WILL YOU ALL SHUT UP?!

YOU SPENT THE NIGHT WITH HIM, RIGHT?
YEAH! YEAH! YEAH!
YOU DID, AND WE'VE GOT PROOF !!

I SLEPT IN THE MANAGER'S ROOM !!
AND YOU REALLY THINK ANYBODY'S GOING TO BUY THAT?!
WHA-?? HAH!

HEE HEE HEE
HAPPY ENGAGEME
BLAH BLAH
YADDA YADDA

YADDA YADDA
SWIP SWIP
YAGAMI

BAM BAM
SKREEK

WHERE ARE WE?
WHO AM I ?

THIS IS A CLASS-ROOM.
AND YOU'RE OUR TEACHER.
KLUNNK
VRRROOM

...AND SO, TODAY...
...MR. GODAI'S STUDENT-TEACHING PERIOD COMES TO A CLOSE.

I WILL HAND OUT FORMS...
...AND YOU WILL WRITE A BRIEF EVALUATION BY THE END OF THE DAY...

...TO BE GIVEN TO YOUR CLASS REPRESEN-TATIVE.

CLASS REPRESENTATIVE. YOU WILL THEN GIVE THEM TO MR. GODAI.
Y-Y-YES'M.
OOOH

I EXPECTED YAGAMI TO GET DEFENSIVE ABOUT BEING TEASED.
I'D SAY SHE WAS JUST... FLUS-TERED.
UH... YEAH.
TAP TAP TAP

LOOKING AT HER, I'D SAY HER ARDOR HAS COOLED CONSIDER-ABLY.
I CAN ONLY HOPE SO...
TAP TAP

FOR MOST OF THE STUDENTS, IT'S NOTHING MORE THAN A WAY TO STIR UP SOME EXCITEMENT.

HA HA HAA... WELL, IT... UHH... DOES THAT...

THIS IS RIDICULOUS.

SUDDENLY IT'S AN "ENGAGEMENT." JUST ANOTHER STUPID PUBLIC EVENT...

AFTER ALL MY SUFFERING IN SILENCE AND LONELI-NESS...
WHO NEEDS THIS CIRCUS ?!?

SIGH IT'S ALMOST START-ING TO FEEL...
...LIKE IT'S NOT WORTH IT ANY MORE.

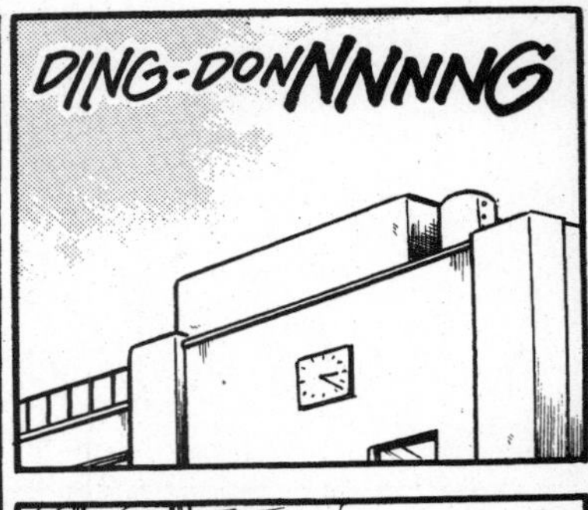
DING-DONNNNNG

SKR-RID-RID

EVERY-BODY FILL OUT AN EVALUA-TION?
I'M TAKIN' 'EM TO MR. GODAI.
GO AHEAD!

YOUR LAST MEET-ING ?
DON'T WASTE IT!
SAY ANY-THING YOU WANT.

STUDENT-TEACHERS' LOUNGE

STAFF
HERE ARE THE EVALUA-TIONS.
THANKS.
STUDENT-TEACHERS LOUNGE

UMM... MR. G...?
YEAH?

......
.....

I'M SORRY FOR ALL THE TROUBLE I CAUSED.
BUT...

I DON'T KNOW WHAT GOT INTO ME.
IT WAS LIKE I WAS OUT OF MY HEAD, OBSESSED OR SOMETHING, AND...

ANYWAY. IT'LL NEVER HAPPEN AGAIN.
UHH... ?

TAKE CARE !
GOOD LUCK !

UM...
SURE.

FUNNY, BUT...

...SORT OF... ANTI-CLIMACTIC.
...HER ENDING IT SO EASILY MADE IT...

...THAT'S HOW IT USUALLY GOES.
BUT I GUESS...
G'BYE !
SEE YA !
HA HA
EE EEK
WHEEE

GOOD LUCK.
TAKE IT EASY, NOW.
THANKS FOR YOUR HELP.

...AND GOOD-BYE TO YOU, TOO, SCHOOL!

YAGAMI...
SHE WAS A NICE GIRL, NOW THAT I THINK ABOUT IT.

I GOT YELLED AT A LOT BECAUSE OF YOU... BUT IT WAS NEVER DULL.
THANKS, KID...

....
......

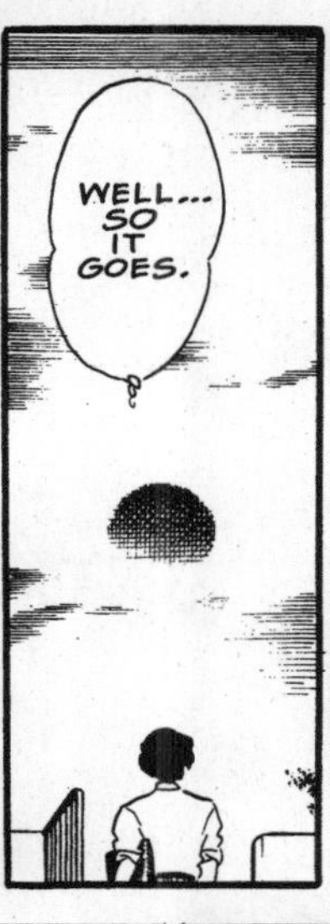
WELL... SO IT GOES.

IT WAS JUST A FEVER, THAT'S ALL...

JUST CALL TO HIM!
COME ON, YAGAMI!
IT'S OKAY...

I'M HOME.
OH, WELCOME BACK.

HUH?
PLIP

...BUT YAGAMI DUMPED ME, SO THAT'S OVER.
UMM...SORRY FOR ALL THE CRAZINESS...

....
....

I DON'T BELI--
...SHE REALLY DID...?

GIRLS THESE DAYS CERTAINLY DON'T MINCE WORDS, DO THEY?
SHE...

YEAH.
...THE SUDDENNESS, I MEAN. AFTER ALL, SHE WAS SO...
...INTENSE ABOUT IT!

I'M NOT CUT OUT TO BE A TEACHER, SO...
"HARD TO UNDERSTAND."
"NERVOUS AND WISHY-WASHY."
KRAKLE

YEAH. BUT I CAN PRETTY MUCH GUESS WHAT THEY WROTE.
TEACHING EVALUATIONS?

......
.....

HEY!
"YOU OWE HER NOW."
LEMME SEE, LEMME SEE...
SQUISH SQUISH SQUISH
PLOP

POP
"PLEASE LOVE YAGAMI FOREVER AND EVER."

"TAKE CARE OF YAGAMI."
"HOW COULD YOU DO IT?"
"MARRY HER SOON."
"INVITE ME TO THE WED-DING!"
COULD YOU
invite Me

ANOTHER... AND ANOTHER...
WEREN'T ANY OF 'EM LISTENING TO ME TEACH?!?
EVI-DENTLY NOT.
YAGAMI'S...
Yagami

PIYO
KRAKLE
THE LONG GOOD-BYE
Farewell FOREVER

A "LONG GOOD-BYE," THEN, IS IT...
??
THE LONG GOOD-BYE

SEE ?
THE CRAZIER THE REST OF THEM GET, THE MORE SENSIBLE SHE IS!

....
....

YOU SEEM DIS-APPOINTED.

I WON-DER...
OH, COME ON! GET REAL !

YA... YA...

SLAM
HI! ANY-BODY HOME ?!?

ONE LI'L CORRECTION...

SKKCH

~~THE~~ SO LONG! GOOD-BYE ~~Farewell FOREVER~~

WELL, MR. G...

SO LONG!!

~~THE~~ SO LONG! GOOD-BYE ~~farewell FOREVER~~

WHAT ELSE COULD I DO, RIGHT?

I MEAN... I ACTUALLY CRIED OVER HIM!

"SO LONG"? NO MORE "FAREWELL FOREVER"?

UH... UH...UH... UHHH...

LUCKY GODAI! SHE'LL BE COMING BACK!!

PART 5

JUST ONE WISH

YOU... WHAT ?!?
HHHHSSSSSSHHH...
GODAI! YOU...
YOU STILL DON'T... ?
DO YOU KNOW HOW LATE IT IS?!
IT'S DECEMBER !
YOU DON'T EVEN HAVE AN OFFER YET?
I NEVER THOUGHT EVEN YOU COULD BE THAT LAZY-- !!
SHUT UP. I'VE MADE IT TO THE FINAL ROUND OF INTERVIEWS FOR FOUR COMPANIES...
...AND I'M WAITING TO HEAR FROM TWO MORE.
BLAH BLAH
MAKING SIX. OR MAKE THAT...
"SICK!"
STUDENT CAFETERIA
HEY, CUT ME SOME SLACK !!
YAMMA YAMMA YAMMA

GEE, THANKS.
YEAH, THEN YOU CAN TAKE ADVANTAGE OF NEXT YEAR'S JOB HUNT.
WHY NOT GO BACK TO SCHOOL ?

GOTTA BE SOME-THING...
......
.....

I GUESS I OUGHTTA TAKE DOWN TWO OR THREE MORE LISTINGS...
NOW HIRING

AND YOU ARE... ??

...IT MUST BE GODAI.

THOSE HUNCHED SHOULDERS, THAT HIDDEN FACE...
NOW HIRING

OH... !
KUROKI. THE PUPPET THEATER CLUB... REMEMBER?

YOU HAVEN'T DROPPED BY THE CLUB ONCE IN THE LAST THREE YEARS.
I'M YOUR PHANTOM MEMBER.
HAVE YOU BEEN IN SCHOOL ALL THIS TIME?
I COULD ASK YOU THE SAME.
SORRY.
IT'S JUST BEEN SO LONG, YOU KNOW?
TINKLE BELL
Cafe

YOU DO HAVE A JOB, RIGHT?
DON'T GIVE ME "HUH," MISTER.
HUH ?
SO HOW'S YOUR FIRST JOB LOOK?
WHAT-EVER...

....
......

"NOT YET"?
WELL, UH... NOT QUITE YET, BUT...

I'VE MADE IT TO THE FINAL ROUND OF INTERVIEWS FOR FOUR COMPANIES...
...AND I'M WAITING TO HEAR FROM TWO MORE!
LOOK, IT MAY NOT BE ALL SET, BUT...

MM.

WITH THAT MANY POLES IN THE WATER, YOU'RE BOUND TO HOOK AT LEAST ONE FISH.
THEN YOU'RE AS GOOD AS EM-PLOYED, AREN'T YOU?

UNTIL THEN, YOU HAVE SOME FREE TIME...
REALLY??
YEAH? YOU THINK SO?
NOTES

WHAT--?! ME... IN A PRESCHOOL CHRISTMAS SHOW...?!?

UH-HUH.
REMEMBER THE PREZ?
YOU MEAN THE... UH...
...HALF-MAN, HALF-BEAST?

HE'S BEEN WORKING AT A PRE-SCHOOL SINCE GRADUATION.

HE AND THE OTHER TEACHERS PLANNED THIS CHRISTMAS SHOW...

...BUT THEN TWO OF THEM CAUGHT COLDS AND LOST THEIR VOICES.
AND I CARE BECAUSE...??

HOW'S YOUR THEN-GIRL-FRIEND DOING?
"GIRL-FRIEND"?
XMAS

YOU KNOW. THE ONE WHO CAME TO THE SCHOOL FESTIVAL, FRESHMAN YEAR...
...AND PLAYED THE PRIN-CESS.
OH. YOU MEAN MY MANAGER.
SNIK

WHATEVER. CAN YOU BRING HER ALONG TOO?
SHE WAS PRETTY GOOD.
ARE YOU NUTS--?!
WE'RE BUSY PEOPLE!!

THERE WILL BE SOME SMALL...
...MONETARY COMPENSATION.

HOW CAN I EVEN CONSIDER IT...?
KA-TA K
KA-TA K
I CAN'T BELIEVE THIS...

...CHRISTMAS "CASH" WILL BE THE LEAST OF MY WORRIES.
HHSSSHH
IF I DON'T GET A REAL JOB...

GODAI! FINALLY! TWO TELE-GRAMS CAME FOR YOU!
WHAT... ??

ONE OF 'EM'S GOTTA COME THROUGH.
HWOOOOOOO
NO, NO, I CAN'T THINK LIKE THAT...

I'M HOME.

THEY MUST BE JOB OFFERS! HERE!
TH- THANKS.

KRAKL

...NOT WITH FOUR CHANCES LEFT.
DON'T WORRY... I'M NOT GONNA HANG MYSELF OR ANYTHING...

DON'T GIVE UP! YOUR LUCK'S BOUND TO TURN!
UMM, UH... GODAI...?
Tp Tp Tp

BRRRRT

NEXT TIME I'LL JUST SAY... "THESE CAME FOR YOU..."
TP TP...

HELLO ?
YES, THIS IS MAISON IKKOKU...
MS. KUROKI...? YES, I'M THE MANAGER, BUT...
......
.....
OH! YES! THE PUPPET THEATER CLUB !
OF COURSE I REMEMBER.
WHAT? CHRISTMAS... ??

WHAT ?
YOU AGREED ?!?
YES... FOR BOTH OF US...
PLEASE COME, GODAI !
IT'LL BE A GOOD DISTRACTION.
UH-HUH.
......
.....
TP TP TP TP

I KNOW SHE'S TRYING TO MAKE ME FEEL BETTER, BUT...
...HAVING TO PUT UP WITH HER PITY ONLY MAKES IT WORSE...
I CAN'T EVEN STAND BEING AROUND HER, NOT HAVING A JOB...
AND YET, HE ACCEPTS HER INVITATION.
HWOOOO... RATTLE
WHAT A WORM.

COME CHRIST-MAS...
BUY IT NOW! BUY IT NOW!
SEASONAL SALE
CHRISTMAS SALE!

HHSSSSHH..
WHEE! EEE!
OKAY, LET'S OPEN OUR SCRIPTS UP...
IT'S AN EASY STORY, SO...
JUST RE-LAX AND...
SCRIPT
DITTO

HE'S SO MISER-ABLE.
MAYBE THIS WASN'T SUCH A GREAT IDEA...
SCHOOL XMAS PLAY! "The Three Wishes"
BUT IF HE JUST SITS AROUND AND MOPES, HE'S ONLY GOING TO MAKE IT ALL WORSE.
IF I CAN GET HIS HEAD OUT OF HIS TROUBLES FOR JUST ONE DAY...

OKAY. NARRATOR.
"IT WAS A COLD, COLD CHRISTMAS EVE..."
"AND A PAUPER WANDERED THE LAND, SEEKING WORK..."
FUMP
FUMP

SOMETHING WRONG?
N-NO... NO...
HUF HUF

OKAY, CUT THE MUSIC.
PAUPER!

"PL-PLEASE GIVE ME A JOB!
I'LL... I'LL DO ANYTHING!"
THAT WAS GOOD, GODAI! REAL FEELING!
"I, HIRE THE LIKES OF YOU? SHOO!"

OKAY, PRINCESS... LET HIM HAVE IT!
HIS MONTH'S SCHEDULE

"Y-YOU WORTHLESS... J-J-JOBLESS... P--P-P..."
HOLD IT, HOLD IT! WHY DO YOU KEEP ON STUMBLING OVER THAT LINE?

MAKE IT ANGRY!!
"YOU WORTHLESS, JOBLESS PAUPER!!"

ALL RIGHT, EVERYBODY. TAKE A FIVE-MINUTE BREAK.
....
....

THEY BRING BACK MEMORIES... DON'T THEY, GODAI?
YOU MADE THESE...
I REMEMBER...

THIS LITTLE GUY USED TO BE A PRINCE...
...BUT NOW HE'S JUST A RAGGED LITTLE...

....
....

OKAY! DID EVERYBODY FINISH THEIR JUICE AND COOKIES ??
NOW IT'S TIME FOR "THE THREE WISHES."
CLAP CLAP
CLAP CLAP
CLAP CLAP

WA HA HA HA
SHOO, PAUPER! SHOO!
A JOB! A JOB! A JOB!
FAPP

OH, WOE... IT'S CHRISTMAS, BUT NO ONE WILL GIVE ME ANY WORK...

GODAI!!
KLUNK
MY DADDY SAYS THAT'S WHAT YOU CALL A "LOSER"!

WHAT SADNESS WEIGHS UPON YOU, YOUNG ONE...?
WHO ARE YOU, SIR...??

THE SPIRIT OF THE CHRISTMAS TREE.
AND EVERY CHRIST-MAS EVE...
...I GRANT A POOR MAN THREE WISHES!

I WISH FOR FOOD!
I'M SO HUNGRY, SPIRIT!
HEE HEE HEE HEE
PLOOP
AS YOU WISH.

SECOND, BRING ME...
...THE PRINCESS WHO LIVES IN THE CASTLE ABOVE!
AS YOU WISH.
DRY ICE

POOOF
YAY! YAY! YAY!

OH! WHERE AM I?
WHO ARE YOU??

WILL YOU MARRY ME, PRINCESS?
DON'T BE ABSURD, YOU... P-P-PAUPER.
PAP
HA HA HA
LOSER! LOSER!

WHAT'S YOUR PROB-LEM?
DID YOUR FRIENDS CALL YOU "PAUPER" WHEN YOU WERE A KID?
NO... IT'S NOT...

DON'T WORRY ABOUT MY FEELINGS.
IT'S OKAY. REALLY.
BUT I'M NOT! I...I...

UH... WE'RE DOING A SHOW HERE...
IF YOU WERE RICH, I WOULD MARRY YOU.
TRULY. PRIN-CESS...??

THEN MY THIRD WISH...
...IS FOR MONEY !!
AS... YOU...

...WISH !
KLONK...
....
......

BUT, SPIRIT... THIS IS BUT A SINGLE COPPER! I NEED MORE!
YOUR WISHES HAVE BEEN GRANTED.
FARE-WELL!

POOF
I'M HUNGRY !
AND I'M FREEZ-ING, TOO... !

Y-Y...
YOU... W-W...

WHAT ?!
YOU CAN'T TREAT ME TO A FEAST ?
OR BUY ME A COAT ?!?

GO RIGHT AHEAD.
YOU WORTH-LESS, JOB-LESS PAUPER !!

AND SO THE PRINCESS RETURED ANGRILY TO HER CASTLE.
MY LOVE!

......
......
LOSER! LOSER!
HA HA A
CLAP CLAP CLAP CLAP

THANKS A LOT!

HM?
'TIS THE SEASON
GODAI... I'M SO SORRY...
XMAS

......
......
Sale

MY TREAT.
HOW 'BOUT A DRINK ON THE WAY HOME?

BUT IF I HADN'T BUTTED IN AND OFFERED--
OH, COME ON, IT'S NOT YOUR FAULT.

REALLY. SOMETIMES IT FEELS GOOD TO BLOW A WHOLE DAY'S BUDGET AT ONCE.
WELL...
BIG CHRISTMAS SALE
ODEN

I REALLY... DON'T KNOW WHAT TO SAY...
I'M SERIOUS! I REALLY DIDN'T MIND!

BESIDES... IT WAS ALL TRUE...

OH, GODAI... PLEASE...
WHAT PRIDE DO I HAVE LEFT TO INJURE?

FORGET THE PRIN-CESS...
I CAN'T EVEN MAKE A... REAL-LIFE WOMAN HAPPY...

....

I THINK IT'S A LITTLE PRE-MATURE TO DECIDE THAT...
BUT I'M SO LOUSY AT RUN-NING MY OWN LIFE!
I'M AL-WAYS A STEP BE-HIND...

...WHY IT ALWAYS ENDS UP LIKE THIS...
I HATE IT, BUT I NEVER KNOW...

YOU DON'T HAVE TO HUMOR ME ANY MORE.
OH, STOP IT--!
...I LOVE.
BUT... THAT'S THE KIND OF PERSON...

PWEEEEEEEEEE
.....
....
KAA KLA KKKA KLA KK

...THE MORE PEOPLE PITY ME... THE MORE PITIFUL I FEEL !!
IT'S LIKE THIS...

MAN. THREE WISHES, HUH?
THAT'D BE SO SWEET, IF IT COULD HAPPEN !!
ODEN

I'M *NOT* HUMOR-ING YOU...
BUT...

EXCEPT MINE'D BE A LOT SMALLER THAN THE PAUPER'S.
JUST A BETTER DEGREE...
A GOOD JOB...
AND THEN...

......
WELL, WE SHOULD PROBABLY START HEADING BACK...
......

UM... KYOKO...
YES?

THERE IS ONE THING...
...ONE WISH I DO HAVE...
THERE... IS... ?
BA-BUMP

WILL YOU...

...LOAN ME SOME MONEY?

PART 6
KIMONO CONNECTION

A JOB AS A BANK RECEPTIONIST, KOZUE?
CONGRATULATIONS!
HEH-HEH... THANKS TO MY DAD'S CONNECTIONS.

PART 6
KIMONO CONNECTION

AAHH, WHAT AN AUSPICIOUS START FOR THE YEAR!
BEAUTIFUL WEATHER... AND THREE BEAUTIFUL LADIES!
SWELL.
THAT YAGAMI GIRL'S A CUTE ONE.
LOOKS LIKE SHE WANTS TO IMPRESS YOU, TOO.
YEAH.
SO WHAT MORE DO YOU NEED TO UNDERSTAND, HUH?!
STAB
WHAT'S WRONG, GODAI?
I CAN SEE BEING DEPRESSED BECAUSE YOU HAVEN'T LANDED A JOB YET, BUT...
SURE! YOU HAVE ALL YEAR TO WORRY ABOUT IT!
THINK HAPPY THOUGHTS!
LET'S FORGET ABOUT THAT FOR TODAY, SHALL WE?

YOU STILL HAVE SHOTS AT THREE COMPANIES, RIGHT?
IT WAS FOUR A COUPLE DAYS AGO...
NOW, THERE YOU GO DRAGGING YOURSELF DOWN AGAIN...
LIQUOR
NEW
SALE

NOW, NOW--
GAAK
PTOO
AND EVEN IF THE OTHER THREE DO REJECT YOU...

WHY NOT?
...JUST BECOME A TEACHER!
HF HF HF HF

WHY DON'T WE TALK ABOUT SOME-THING ELSE...

YEAH, CHEER UP!
ONE OF MY FRIENDS JUST TOOK A TEACHING JOB AFTER YEARS OF REJECTION!
UM... SOMETHING ELSE...
JUST RELAX.
YOU'LL FIND SOMETHING!

DON'T YOU HAVE ANOTHER INTERVIEW WITH MITSUTOMO? YOUR FIRST CHOICE?
YEAH... FOR A SECOND-LEVEL JOB.
MITSUTOMO ENTERPRISES?

WOW...
YOU'RE GONNA JOIN THEM, MR. G?
IF THEY LET ME, YEAH.
.....
?
HEE HEE
YOU SEEM AWFULLY PLEASED, YAGAMI...

'CAUSE MY DAD'S THE PERSONNEL MANAGER OF MITSUTOMO ENTERPRISES!
BUT OF COURSE!

Y-Y--
I'VE BEEN WONDERING WHAT YOU'D DO IF I SAID THAT!

NOT LIKE YAGAMI WOULD BE A GOOD CONNECTION ANYWAY...
EVEN WITH NO CONNECTIONS.
OH, YOU'LL BE FINE...

NOT FUNNY.
YOU WERE JOKING...??

SPARE ME THE SAR-CASM.
A-HA-HAA!
THE RECIPIENT OF THE HOPE, TRUST, AND CONCERN OF ALL THESE BEAUTIFUL LADIES!
WHAT A LUCKY FELLOW YOU ARE, GODAI!

NOW, REALLY, EVERY-BODY...
...CAN'T WE FIND SOME-THING *ELSE*?

OF COURSE. HMM...

OH, YES! KOZUE, DID I HEAR THAT YOU FOUND A JOB? CONGRATULATIONS!
THANKS! IT'S SO GREAT!

EXTRA HOT TABASCO
BOURBON Fine Drinkin

HM?
WHAT'S HAPPENED TO OUR MISS YAGAMI?
IT *HAS* BEEN A WHILE.

PER-HAPS SHE'S NOT FEEL-ING WELL?
I'LL GO CHECK ON HER.

LADIES
TOBACCO
HWURRRLL
KOFF
YAGAMI
?
LADIES

POOR DEAR... WHAT HAPPENED??
JUST STARTED FEELING... ALL FAINT...
HUKK...

YOU NEED AIR. LOOSEN YOUR KIMONO.
NO!!
SHHHHH

THEN MR. G MIGHT NEVER GET A JOB...
WHAT?

YAGAMI DEAR, YOU'RE NOT MAKING ANY SENSE!
MY DAD'S REALLY STRICT!

BESIDES, WHAT'S THAT HAVE TO DO WITH GODAI...
...GET-TING... A... ??

...HE'LL THINK MR. GODAI DRAGGED ME INTO A LOVE HOTEL OR SOMETHING!
IF I SHOW UP WITH MY CLOTHES ALL LOOSE...
YOU'VE BEEN READING THE TABLOIDS TOO MUCH!

....
....

UM... I UNDERSTAND YOUR FEELINGS. BUT THINK ABOUT IT...

IF MR. GODAI MAKES A GOOD IMPRES-SION...
BUT MY FATHER NEVER FORGETS A FACE...
HAHH HAHH...

IT'S MR. G'S BIG CHANCE.
THEN IT'S TRUE...? YOUR FATHER REALLY WORKS AT...?

EVEN IF GODAI IS HIS DAUGHTER'S FAVORITE STUDENT-TEACHER...
...IS THAT REALLY ANY REASON FOR YOUR FATHER TO HIRE HIM?
THAT'S WHY HE'S GOTTA MEET MY DAD FACE-TO-FACE! SO THEY CAN BOND!
JANITOR

I MEAN... WHAT'S HE GOT TO LOSE ??
WELL... THAT'S TRUE...

GODAI... CAN I... ?
YEAH ?

HUH? ESCORT YAGAMI HOME... ?!
SHE REALLY IS SICK... AND... UHH... HER FATHER...

...IT TURNS OUT SHE WASN'T JOKING AFTER ALL.
SHE...

SO, IF YOU...
FOR-GET IT.

SO...
?
FINE. SO...
?

I MAY BE GRASPING AT STRAWS...
...BUT I'M NOT KISSING AT BUTTS!

HUH... HUH...
DON'T YOU HAVE SOME OBLIGATION?
SO, YOUR GUEST AND FORMER STUDENT IS SICK.
.....
...

ACTING LIKE HIS WIFE !!
GEEZ, LOOK AT HER... !
OKAY.
...AND GIVE HIM A FIRM HELLO!
JUST CARRY YOURSELF WITH CONFIDENCE...

GOOD LUCK.
ALL RIGHT, ALL RIGHT!
C'MON, MR. G! BEFORE I PASS OUT!

VRROOOOOOOM!

BUT MY DAD NEVER FORGETS A FACE... IF MR. GODAI...
...MAKES A GOOD IMPRESSION...
IF ONLY I HAD HER FAITH...

OH, WELL. I GUESS IT COULDN'T BE HELPED.

I'M NOT CUT OUT FOR THIS WHOLE KISS-UP THING...
I DON'T EVEN THINK IT'S RIGHT...

...AND SPLIT.
I'LL JUST DUMP HER ON THE DOOR-STEP...

...HAVE TO LEAVE YOU RIGHT HERE.
BUT I'LL...

I'M SORRY, YAGAMI...
HERE YOU GO.
SKREE

......
....
VROOOM

I'M SORRY, MR. G.
I REALLY CAN'T WALK RIGHT NOW!
......
....

YEAH, LIKE HELL I CAN'T...

BUT YOU'RE GONNA MEET MY DAD...
...ONE WAY OR ANOTHER!
DING-DONG

HEY, TEACH?
NOW'S THE TIME TO BE ASSERTIVE!
HUH?

MY FATHER'S PRETTY HARD-LINE.
HE HATES SLACKERS, Y'KNOW?
WHAT?!

WHY SHOULD I CARE??
IT'S NOT LIKE I WANT TO...

KLIK
HUT!

IBUKI!! WHAT'S THE MATTER ?!?
H-H-HELLO !!
Y-YOUR DAUGHTER WASN'T FEELING VERY W-WELL, SO...
SAVE THE ASSERTIVENESS, MR. G.
THAT'S MY MOM.
NOT MY DAD.
OH, DEAR...
I'M SO SORRY TO HAVE TROUBLED YOU...
OH. WEREN'T YOU A STUDENT TEACHER AT...
YES, MA'AM.
WHERE'S DAD ?
WON'T YOU COME IN?
IF YOU'LL FORGIVE ME, I'LL...
DON'T YOU DARE WEASEL OUT, NOT NOW!
NO, REALLY, I... I...

DAD, GUESS WHAT?
MR. GODAI'S APPLYING AT MITSU-TOMO!
H-HEY!

JUST BE QUIET!
BUT... BUT...

COME ALONG, DEAR. IT'S TIME TO CHANGE...

SO. YOU'VE APPLIED TO MITSU-TOMO.
YES... BUT...

DON'T GET ME WRONG, SIR.
I DIDN'T HAVE ANY ULTERIOR MOTIVE IN BRINGING YOUR DAUGHTER HOME.

WHAT DO YOU MEAN BY THAT?!

I JUST MEAN...
...I WASN'T TRYING TO WIN YOUR FAVOR THROUGH HER, THAT'S ALL.
......
......

WHAT'S YOUR NAME, SON?
MY...?

GO-- GODAI.

GODAI. I'LL REMEMBER THAT.
HUH?

YOU SEEM LIKE A PRETTY AWKWARD, BUMBLING KID...
...BUT SOMETIMES THERE'S MORE PROMISE IN YOUR TYPE THAN IN THE SLICK ONES!

I LOOK FORWARD TO SEEING YOU AT THAT INTER-VIEW!
UH... WHA--

THANK YOU, SIR!

SLAM...
GASP

HIC

I'M BACK!

AND... ?? HOW DID IT GO?

WELL... I DON'T THINK I LEFT A BAD IMPRES-SION...
...BUT I REALLY DON'T THINK I IMPROVED MY CHANCES AT ALL.

EXCEPT HE KNOWS ME NOW!
HE KNOWS ME!

IBUKI! SHOULDN'T YOU BE RESTING?
I'M FINE, I'M FINE, I'M FINE!
TMP
TMP

DAD!
WAKE UP! COME ON!
SHNAX

HUH ?!
GODAI ??
WHOOZAT ?!? IBUKI, WHENJOO GET HOME? HIC
YOU MEAN, YOU DON'T REMEMBER ANY-THING?!
GIVE UP, HONEY. YOUR FATHER'S BEEN SCHNOCKERED SINCE THIS MORNING.

PART 7

BIRTH IS NEVER AS HARD AS THE WORRYING

YAMMA YAMMA YAMMA
....
....
SO HE ESCORTED YOU HOME ON NEW YEAR'S DAY.
WHAT DOES THAT HAVE TO DO WITH HIS INTERVIEW?
BRRRT BRRRT BRRRT
BUT, DAD, YOU MET HIM! AND LIKED HIM!
YOU'VE GOT TO REMEMBER!
I TOLD YOU. I DON'T.
IN ANY CASE...
...I'M NOT SURE I LIKE A MAN WHO'D ASK MY DAUGHTER TO HELP--
BUT HE DIDN'T!!

HE'S OBVIOUSLY USING YOU TO GET A JOB...
...AND I DON'T THINK YOU SHOULD ASSOCIATE WITH--
THEN DON'T STICK YOUR NOSE WHERE IT DOESN'T BELONG!

I CAN'T WAIT TO SEE HIM COME SAUNTERING INTO THAT INTER-VIEW.
I'LL TEACH HIM A THING OR TWO.
MR. GODAI'S NOT LIKE THAT!
YOU'VE GOT IT ALL WRONG, DAD!

FINE, THEN! BE AN IDIOT!!

THIS WASN'T HOW IT WAS SUPPOSED TO GO...
MR. GODAI, I'M SO SORRY...

BRRRING
BRRRING
BRRRING

I'M COMING, I'M COMING!
TM TM TM
HELLO, MAISON IKKOKU--
HUF HUF

THE WIDOW !!

UMM... IS MR. GODAI THERE...?
OH... IS THAT YOU, MISS YAGAMI?
PIYO PIYO

GODAI'S NOT IN RIGHT NOW...
...BUT IF YOU'D LIKE TO LEAVE A MESSAGE...
PIYO PIYO

KLIK

WELL!
SHE ONLY GETS STRANGER!
CHINGG

....
......

THE PERSONNEL MANAGER?! OF MITSU-TOMO?! HIS HOUSE?!?
YEEE-UP! AND HE LIKED ME, TOO! HEH HEH HEHHH!
GLASSES CONTACTS

YOU DOG, YOU!
USING HIS DAUGHTER JUST TO...
WELL, LET'S REMEMBER THIS DOESN'T GUARANTEE ANYTHING.

BUT I'M BETTING I LEAVE THAT INTER-VIEW...
...WITH A JOB IN MY HAND!

YAGAMI. CUTTING AGAIN.
SHE HAD TO LEAVE EARLY!

IS YAGAMI HERE?
YAGAMI?

HWWOOOOOOOOOOOoo
TP TP TP TP

HWWOOOOOOOOO

I NEVER BELIEVED IN GOD... OR GODS...

SO PLEASE TAKE CARE OF MR. GODAI!

GONG GONG

MAY SUCCESS BE HIS...

HWOOOOOOO

---HWWOOOOOOOOOooo°o
......
......
YAGAMI...
?
VWIP
......
......
MAISON IKKOKU
.....
?

SHF
SHF

YAGAMI
!
VWIP

FWAP
FWAP

THERE'S NO POINT IN YOUR PACING HERE IN THE COLD...
I REALLY DON'T KNOW WHEN GODAI WILL BE BACK.

WHY DON'T YOU COME IN AND WAIT IN MY ROOM, OKAY?
......
......

UM...

CAN... CAN YOU PLEASE GIVE THIS TO MR. GODAI ?
MR. G
YAGAMI

IT'S AN AMULET I BOUGHT AT A SHRINE.
ON
KU

PLEASE TELL HIM I SAID...
...HE SHOULD MEET TOMORROW'S INTERVIEW... WITH DETERMINATION.

DID SOMETHING HAPPEN?
....
MAISON
KOKU

BUT...
YAGAMI!!?
'BYE!

MAISON
IKKOKU

....

THE BIG DAY.

WELL, I'M OFF !!

OH, GODAI... ?

YES?

THIS IS FOR YOU... MISS YAGAMI DELIVERED IT YESTERDAY.

OH.

MR. G. YAGAMI

....
....

MR. G. YAGAMI

Safe Birth

SHE SAID IT WOULD BRING SUC-CESS.

RATTLE
R.G.
GAMI

WHY NOT TAKE IT? "THE THOUGHT THAT COUNTS," AND ALL THAT.
GEEZ... WHAT A SCATTER-BRAIN!
AND WHAT'S *THAT* SUP-POSED TO MEAN?
"SAFE BIRTH"... ??
G.
GAMI

DON'T WORRY! I'LL BE FINE!
REMEM-BER... DETERMI-NATION!

THANKS. I'LL GIVE IT MY BEST.
AND... AND FACE THAT INTER-VIEW WITH DETERMI-NATION.

BONK
I WON-DER...
MAISON IKKOKU

HE SHOULD BE LEAVING FOR THE INTERVIEW AROUND NOW...
I HOPE THAT WIDOW PASSED THAT GOOD LUCK THING ON TO HIM...
MR. GODAI...
I'LL BE PRAYING FOR YOU.
OH, *PLEASE* DON'T LET MY DAD CRUSH HIM...!!
Mitsutomo Enterprises
WHAT KIND OF ANIMAL WOULD USE A MAN'S ONLY PRECIOUS DAUGHTER? THE CHILD WHO CAME TO HIM SO LATE IN LIFE?
WELL, I'LL SHOW HIM THE RAGE OF A *FATHER WRONGED*!!
...TRANSFER STATION FOR THE YAMANOTE LINE...
I'M RUNNING FIVE MINUTES LATE...
TRAIN ARRIVING

HOPEFULLY I CAN STILL GET THERE HALF AN HOUR EARLY AND PREPARE MYSELF...

I COULD TAKE A SHORT-CUT THROUGH THE BACK STREETS...
MITSUTOMO
BELL

TMP TMP TMP TMP

OKAY... I'M PRETTY SURE I TURN RIGHT HERE...
DENTIST
THIS'LL PUT ME ON THE STREET RIGHT IN FRONT OF THE MITSUTOMO BUILDING...

DETERMI-NATION !!
I WONDER IF KYOKO IS REALLY COUNT-ING ON ME...

WELL, I'LL GIVE IT EVERY-THING I'VE GOT!
AND WHEN I GET THIS JOB...

...I'LL PRO-POSE TO HER !
MY WHOLE LIFE DEPENDS ON THIS INTER-VIEW!!

THLY
ARKING
LOANS
REALTORS
TUP

UM...
ARE YOU ALL RIGHT ??
C-C... CAB...

WHAT ?
NTHLY KING
GET A CAB... FOR ME... P-P-PLEASE...

MY... MY WATERS BROKE... EARLY...
HUH HUH
NTHLY
Y-Y-YOU MEAN... A BABY ?!?

IT... IT'S COMING !
UNNHH...

HURRY !!
AT... AT THE INTER-SECTION !!
G-GOT IT!
NTHLY KING

THERE'S GOTTA BE A PHONE AROUND HERE SOME-WHERE!
LOANS
REALTORS

VI NG&LOAN
BANK
VOOM
BEEEEEP

BLAST IT!!
Buuuuump
BEEEEEP
THEY'RE ALL TAKEN !!
TEA
TAXI

I... I HAVE TO HURRY...
MY INTER-VIEW... !

AN AMBU-LANCE !!

YES... YES! THE BABY'S COMING !!
SHE'S AT...

NNNH NNNHH
TMP TMP

YOU'LL BE OKAY NOW!
I CALLED AN AMBU-LANCE!
LISTEN, I GOTTA GO, SO...
ZEEH ZEEH

P-P-PLEASE... DON'T LEAVE ME...
YOU CAN'T...
B-B-BUT...

IT'S MY FIRST... BABY.
DON'T LEAVE ME HERE... ALL ALONE...

Y-YOU DON'T UNDER-STAND!
NNGH
NNGH
I-I-I'VE GOT AN INTER-VIEW...

M-MA'AM! LOOK! IT'S HERE!
WEEEOO
WEEEOO

BAM
KLAK
KLAK
KLAK

YOU'RE THE FATHER, RIGHT?!
BETTER COME WITH US!
HUH?!

NO! NO!!
I WAS JUST... I WAS JUST...

DON'T ABAN-DON ME...
PLEASE! L-LET GO! LET...
MONTH
PARKIN
ZEEEH
ZEEEH
ZEEEH

I HAVE AN INTER-VIEW!!
NO! NO!!
FUMP
SHUMP
WOOM

WEEEOO WEEEOO WEEEOO
VRROOOM
LET ME GO!

...OR HE'LL GET A JOB. AND THAT GIRL WILL HAVE HIM IN HER DEBT.
HE'LL EITHER FAIL...
OH, WELL...

FIVE TO TWO.
HE'S ABOUT TO START.

PLEASE HELP MR. GODAI...
GOD... BUDDHA... LADY LUCK...

"BIRTH IS NEVER AS HARD AS THE WORRY-ING..."
NO POINT IN WORRYING ABOUT IT.

W-WEEEEEEOOOO
OPEN UP! LET ME OUT!

WILL YOU PLEASE SETTLE DOWN?!
BAM
WAAAH! WE'RE GOING THE OPPOSITE DIRECTION !!
BAM

MITSUTOMO

IN-DEED.
MR. YAGAMI... WE SHOULD START THE INTER-VIEWS...
KRAK KRAK KRAK

DON'T I LOOK ALL RIGHT?
UMM... ARE YOU ALL RIGHT?

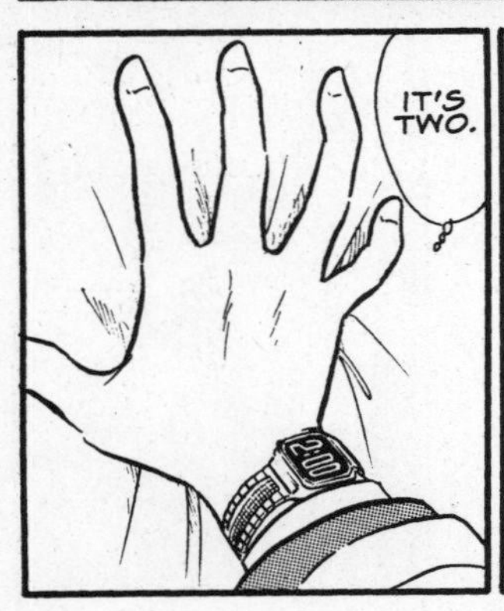
IT'S TWO.

??
I'M... FINISHED...

SLIP...

PACH...
Safe Birth

......
......
OH...
OHHH-
HHH...

HERE YOU GO... MA'AM...
HAHH HAHH
...TO PROTECT THE BABY.

TH--THANKS.

...AND THAT CONCLUDES TODAY'S INTER-VIEWS.
MITS

WAIT... WHAT ABOUT THE ONE CALLED GODAI...?
HUH?

WE HAVE HIM AS A NO-SHOW.
SOME NERVE HE'S GOT... GIVING US THE BRUSH-OFF!
......
......

MR. YAGAMI...??
TP TP TP

FIRST GENERAL HOSPITAL
HWAAAH!
HWAAAAH!

HOW DARE YOU RUN AWAY!!
HOW DARE YOU, YUSAKU GODAI!!
FWOOSH
SQUEEZE

IVERY
CONGRATU-LATIONS! IT'S A BOY!
AND ONE OF THE EASIEST LABORS I'VE SEEN!
WOW... LUCKY ME...
HWAAAHH!

PART 8
POST-PARTUM DEPRESSION

MITSUTOMO
MITSUTOMO ENTERPRISES
......
BOSS
BEEP
HONK
B-BEEP

RESUME INFORMATION
No.
GODAI, YUS
Birth Register
D.O.B.:
AGE: 23 YEARS
Prefecture
Phone No. (Area code)
CLOCK HILL 2-6-5

SO, YUSAKU GODAI... TIME AND AGAIN YOU INFURIATE ME!
IT'S MOST ANNOYING THAT YOU WOULD MISS THIS INTER-VIEW, WHEN I'VE BEEN WAITING ESPECIALLY FOR YOU!

THERE WERE A LOT OF THINGS I WANTED TO SAY TO YOU, BOY!
DAMN IT !!
WHAM

WHHSSSH

......

EVEN IF I EX-PLAINED TO THEM WHY I WAS LATE...
...IT'S PROBABLY NO USE.

A GREAT COMPANY LIKE MITSU-TOMO... ≥SIGH.≤ THAT DREAM DIDN'T LAST LONG...
EH ?!

IT'S THAT DAMN KID!

MAY AS WELL JUST GO HOME.
TMP TMP TMP TMP
HEY, YOU! WAIT !

KLIK KLIK

WHSSSSHHH
DAMN IT ALL !!

YOU COWARD !
YOU DID IT AGAIN !

WHAT?! HE DIDN'T SHOW UP AT THE INTER-VIEW ?!?

WH-WHY NOT ?!
HOW THE HELL SHOULD I KNOW ?

SO... NO MATTER HOW FINE A FELLOW YOU CLAIM HE IS, IF HE CAN'T EVEN KEEP AN INTERVIEW APPOINT-MENT...
...HE'S CLEARLY NOT QUALIFIED TO BECOME A BUSINESS-MAN.

BUT, DAD! THERE'S GOT TO BE A GOOD REASON WHY, I JUST KNOW IT!

AW, DAD! CAN'T YOU DO SOMETHING ABOUT IT?!
NOTHING HE CAN SAY NOW COULD POS-SIBLY MAKE A DIFFER-ENCE.

WELL, I'M GOING TO FIND OUT WHAT HAP-PENED!

WAIT! IBUKI, DEAR, IT'S SUPPER-TIME!
HMF. LET HER GO!
SWOOSH

WHY, MR. G?!
WHAT COULD HAVE HAPPENED ?
TMP TMP TMP

OH, MRS. ICHI-NOSE!
WHAT'S GOING ON, GUYS?

IT'S GODAI-- HE CAME HOME, BUT HE'S LOCKED HIMSELF IN HIS ROOM FOR SOME REASON.
PIYO PIYO

I'M REALLY NOT SURE.
MAYBE HE SCREWED UP BIG-TIME AT THE INTERVIEW? Y'THINK ?

WHEN I ASKED HIM HOW IT WENT...
...HE SAID, "IT WAS A SMOOTH DE-LIVERY."

HRM.
SO, LIKE, WOULDN'T THAT MEAN THE INTERVIEW WENT GREAT?
THEN WHY IS HE ACTING SO DEPRESSED?

WHAM
SORRY, BUT THE FRONT DOOR WAS OPEN!
WHERE'S MR. GODAI ?!
YAGAMI ? WHA--
WHAT ARE YOU DOING HERE?
MR. G!! IT'S ME, YAGAMI !!
BAM BAM

WHY DIDN'T YOU GO TO YOUR INTERVIEW ?!?
YOU'VE GOT TO TELL ME!
HE WHAT ?!

GODAI!! IS THIS TRUE ?!?
OPEN THIS DOOR RIGHT NOW!!
PIYO

C'MON, TEACH! OPEN UP!!
BAM BAM BAM
GODAI! PLEASE!
GEEZ LOUISE!

...HOW AM I SUPPOSED TO SIT HERE AND WALLOW IN SELF-PITY AND DISGUST WITH ALL THIS RACKET GOING ON?
DAMN IT ALL...

COME ON! WE'VE GOTTA GO GO GO!!
...I'M SETTING ASIDE TONIGHT TO SIT QUIETLY BY MYSELF AND BITTERLY REPENT THAT ASPECT OF MY PERSONALITY THAT ALLOWS ME TO GET DRAGGED INTO THINGS.
NO MATTER WHAT HAP-PENS...
BAM BAM BAM

Y-Y-YOU'RE RIGHT...
IT'S WEIRDLY QUIET IN THERE, ISN'T IT?

GODAI'S LOCKED IN HIS ROOM?
YAGAMI! DON'T EVEN THINK SUCH A TERRIBLE THING!
MAYBE MR. GODAI'S GONNA KILL HIMSELF!!
PIYO PIYO

HOW ABOUT I BREAK DOWN THE DOOR?
I-I SUPPOSE SO, IN THIS CASE...
PIYO

ONE, TWO--
WHOOSH
WHA AM

GODAI !
MR. G!!
SEE? I'M ALIVE !
I'M ALIVE, SO PLEASE LET ME ALONE, OKAY?!

WHAM
5

....
PIYO PIYO

IT'S... IT'S ALL MY FAULT, I JUST KNOW IT...

BECAUSE I STUCK MY NOSE IN WHERE IT DIDN'T BELONG AND MADE MY FATHER ANGRY...
MR. GODAI PROBABLY PICKED UP ON THAT, AND...
PIYO PIYO

WHAT ARE YOU TALKING ABOUT?
HOW COULD HE HAVE "PICKED UP ON THAT" IF HE DIDN'T EVEN GO TO THE INTERVIEW?!
BECAUSE... BECAUSE... I CAN'T THINK OF ANY OTHER REASON WHY!
PIYO

I'M SORRY, MR. GODAI! I'M REALLY REALLY SORRY!
WAAAAAH
WAH WAHH
OH, FOR GOD'S SAKE, YAGAMI! YOU'RE ACTING LIKE A CHILD!
MR. YAGAMI IS MAD AT ME...?
WHAT THE HECK...?!

THE YAGAMI RESIDENCE

TIK TOK

CURSE THAT GIRL!
SHE'S LATE!
HA HA HA HA

...
MR. GODAI, TAKE ME AWAY FROM ALL THIS! PLEASE!
AHH, MY DARLING YAGAMI!

MY FATHER IS SUCH A HEARTLESS, THOUGHTLESS OLD FOOL! THERE'S NOTHING FOR ME HERE ANYMORE!

MR. YAGAMI IS INDEED MY MORTAL ENEMY!
SO I'LL TAKE HIS PRECIOUS DAUGHTER...

...TO DO WITH HER AS I WISH, AND THEN, WHEN I TIRE OF HER, SELL HER TO THE HIGHEST BIDDER!
NYAHAHAHA

DOOM

TIK TIK TIK TIK

HELLO, MATSUI? WORKING OVER-TIME, EH?!
NO, NO, NO PROBLEM. ER... DO YOU REMEMBER THAT STUDENT WHO DIDN'T SHOW UP TO HIS INTER-VIEW TODAY?
YUSAKU GODAI-- THAT'S HIM. DO YOU HAVE HIS ADDRESS HANDY?

I'LL BE RIGHT BACK.
OH... YOU'RE GOING OUT, HONEY?

VRRROOOOOOOOOOSSSHHHHH

OH, MY... !

LORD, KEEP HER SAFE AND SOUND UNTIL HER FATHER GETS THERE!
IBUKI, MY ONLY DAUGHTER, YOU'RE BEING DECEIVED!

...BUT MY DAD... H-HE...
MR. GODAI'S T-T-TOTALLY INNOCENT, B-BUT...

Y-YEAH... DAD'S TOTALLY CONVINCED!
HE THINKS GODAI SEDUCED YOU AND IS TAKING ADVANTAGE OF YOU...?
PIYO PIYO

SKREEEECH
SLAM

AH!

BONK

IBUKI ?!?
GET LOST, YOU OLD FART!
WHO ASKED YOU TO SHOW UP?!

YOUNG LADY, YOU GET DOWN HERE RIGHT NOW!
YOU'RE COMING HOME WITH ME!

HAH! I'D RATHER DIE THAN LIVE THERE ANYMORE!
YAGAMI, WAIT! STOP!
DETERGENT

GODAI, YOU'VE GOT TO COME OUT AND HELP!
MR. YAGAMI'S HERE AND--
BAM BAM
WHAT?!

HOW ABOUT THIS?
GREAT! THANKS!

YAGAMI! WHOA! WHOA!!

RRG!

ALL RIGHT, GODAI! JUST WHAT THE HELL ARE YOU UP TO, ANYWAY?!

HUH?

FIRST YOU SEDUCE MY INNOCENT DAUGHTER!
YOU'RE A PATHETIC EXCUSE FOR A HUMAN BEING!
THEN YOU ARROGANTLY FAIL TO SHOW UP FOR YOUR INTER-VIEW!
AND NOW YOU'VE TAKEN MY DAUGHTER HOSTAGE! WHAT THE HELL ARE YOU PLANNING TO DO NEXT, YOU SWINE?!

"HOS-TAGE," HE SAYS!
WHAT IN THE WORLD IS THAT OLD GUY BABBLING ABOUT?
WANT I SHOULD THROW THIS HAMMER AT 'IM?
GRAB A BRAIN, AKEMI!

LOOK, YOU MIGHT AS WELL COME IN, MR. YAGAMI.
.....
TAKK

GIVE ME BACK MY DAUGHTER IMMEDI-ATELY.
BUT I NEVER TOOK HER!

IBUKI !!
I'M NOT GOING HOME! NYAH NYAH !

DON'T YOU REALIZE YOU'RE BEING DE-CEIVED ?!
WHAT CAN YOU POSSIBLY SEE IN SUCH A WORTH-LESS, UN-TRUST-WORTHY--

JUST A MOMENT, PLEASE! WHAT I'M HEARING HERE IS TERRIBLY ONE-SIDED, DON'T YOU THINK?

MANAGER...?
AND I DON'T MUCH LIKE THIS "WORTHLESS, UNTRUSTWORTHY" BIT. I MEAN, YOU DON'T EVEN KNOW HIM AT ALL!

YEAH--IF YOU GOT TO KNOW HIM BETTER, YOU'D LEARN HE'S EVEN MORE WORTHLESS AND UNTRUSTWORTHY THAN YOU THOUGHT!
YOU SHUT UP!!

BUT, MANAGER, IT'S REALLY NOT NECESSARY TO YELL AT--
THEN WHY DON'T YOU GET A LITTLE ANGRY?!
YOU'RE THE ONE WHO'S BEING PICKED ON HERE, YOU KNOW!
IN ANY CASE...

...WHY DID YOU RUN AWAY FROM YOUR INTERVIEW?
I THINK I DESERVE TO KNOW THAT MUCH.

I DID NOT "RUN AWAY," SIR! I--

SEE? SEE?! IT'S ALL YOUR FAULT, DAD--
--FOR JUMPING TO YOUR STUPID CONCLUSIONS! BESIDES, I WASN'T SEDUCED AT ALL! I ASKED MR. GODAI TO--
YOU KEEP YOUR MOUTH SHUT!!

UMM... EXCUSE ME? SORRY TO INTERRUPT THINGS...
...BUT IS THERE A "GODAI" LIVING HERE?
HUH?

UH, YEAH...MY NAME IS GODAI, BUT...
OH!

I... I REALLY WANT TO THANK YOU FOR HELPING OUT MY WIFE THIS AFTERNOON. I MEAN, WHAT YOU DID...

HMM? WHAT DO YOU MEAN?
WELL, UM, Y'SEE...
EARLIER TODAY MY WIFE SUDDENLY WENT INTO LABOR AND JUST COLLAPSED ON THE SIDEWALK.

BUT LUCKILY A KIND-HEARTED PASSERBY HELPED HER AND EVEN WENT WITH HER ALL THE WAY TO THE HOSPITAL!
AFTER SHE WAS OKAY, HE LEFT WITHOUT TELLING HER HIS NAME.

BUT WHEN I HEARD THAT HE HAD KEPT SAYING SOMETHING ABOUT THE COMPANY MITSUTOMO ENTERPRISES...
...I CONTACTED THE FIRM AND DISCOVERED THAT...
...TODAY ONE OF THEIR JOB APPLICANTS HAD MYSTERIOUSLY NOT SHOWN UP FOR HIS INTERVIEW.

I KNOW IT'S TERRIBLY LATE...
...BUT I WANTED TO THANK YOU AS SOON AS POS-SIBLE.
I SEE.
PIYO

THEY SAID THAT IF SHE HAD BEEN LEFT ALONE, SHE MAY NOT HAVE MADE IT THROUGH SAFELY...
Y--YOU SAVED MY WIFE AND MY SON!
B-BUT I JUST...

BUT...IF THAT WAS WHAT HAD HAPPENED, WHY DIDN'T YOU SAY SOMETHING SOONER, GODAI?
BE-CAUSE...

IF I HADN'T LET MYSELF GET SHOVED INTO THE AMBULANCE LIKE THAT...
...I WOULD HAVE MADE IT ON TIME!
...BE-CAUSE IT WAS NO EX-CUSE.

.....

YOUNG GODAI...
...IT SEEMS I HAVE CRUELLY MIS-UNDERSTOOD YOU.
HUH?

IF YOU WERE THE KIND OF FELLOW WHO WOULD ABANDON A DESPERATE WOMAN IN LABOR IN ORDER TO MAKE IT TO AN INTERVIEW...
...I WOULD HAVE DES-PISED YOU FROM THE BOTTOM OF MY HEART, BUT...

Y-YEAH... EVEN INSIDE THE AMBULANCE, HE CONTINUED TO COMFORT MY WIFE. HE EVEN GAVE HER A "SAFE BIRTH" AMULET FROM A LOCAL TEMPLE...
...TO PROTECT THE BABY DURING DELIVERY.
I SEE. YES, INDEED!
SNFF

THERE! NOW DO YOU UNDERSTAND, DAD?
THAT'S THE KIND OF PERSON MR. GODAI IS!
YES, AND IN THIS DAY AND AGE WHEN SO MANY PEOPLE ARE SELF-CENTERED...
...YOU ARE A TRULY WONDERFUL PERSON.
JUST THE SORT OF HONEST, DECENT, PROMISING PERSON WE NEED AT MITSUTOMO.
EH ?!

DAD...
Y-Y-YOU MEAN...
??
??

AHH, IT'S A CRYING SHAME...
BUT, SADLY...

PIYO PIYO

RRRGGH!

THE INTERVIEW PERIOD IS CLOSED-- THERE'S NOTHING I CAN DO ABOUT IT.
WHAT DO YOU--
JUST ONE SECOND, DAD.

UNFORTUNATELY, THAT IS A COMPLETELY SEPARATE MATTER.
BUT YOU JUST SAID THAT MITSUTOMO NEEDS PEOPLE LIKE MR. GODAI!

UHH... THANKS.
...ANYWAY, I'D LIKE YOU TO HAVE THIS CAKE AS A TOKEN OF MY THANKS.
WAIT! IBUKI!!
DA DA DA DA DA

DADADADADADA
IBU-KI!
MISS YA-GAMI!

SLAM
KCHAK
HEY, WAIT! THAT'S--

YOU BETTER LISTEN, DAD! UNTIL YOU FIX UP A JOB FOR MR. GODAI...
...I'M NOT COMING HOME!!

IBUKI YAGAMI! THAT IS MY ROOM!
IBUKI, YOU GET OUT OF THERE RIGHT NOW!
HO HO... IT WOULD BE MOST APPRO-PRIATE FOR IT TO BE A BIRTH-DAY CAKE, YES?

PART 9

THE MIDNIGHT INTERVIEW

MAISON IKKOKU "HOSTAGE" CRISIS: DAY THREE.
MRS. OTONASHI, I'M BORROWING THE VACUUM CLEANER, 'KAY?
CHAK
OH, GOOD MORNING, MR. G!
HEY! MY SHIRT!
OH, YEAH... SORRY 'BOUT THAT. I SHOULD'VE ASKED, HUH?
I KINDA DIDN'T BRING ANY CLOTHES WITH ME WHEN I CAME, SO...
MR. G, REALLY, IF YOU WANT TO COME BACK WITH ME TO ROOM FIVE...
...DON'T BE SHY! I DON'T MIND!
PIYO PIYO
PIYO PIYO

MANAGER, LOOK... I'M REALLY SORRY TO CAUSE YOU SO MUCH TROUBLE...
OH NO, DON'T WORRY ABOUT ME.
I CAN DEAL WITH IT, BUT...
WELL, OF ALL THE NERVE!
WHOSE ROOM DOES SHE THINK IT IS, ANYWAY ?!
PIYO PIYO
SHE REALLY IS A BOTHER, ISN'T SHE?
...SINCE SHE'S PRETTY MUCH TAKEN OVER YOUR ROOM.
...IT MUST REALLY BE A PAIN FOR YOU...

WE REALLY HAVE A BIT OF A PROB-LEM HERE, DON'T WE?
NO KIDDING! I'M NOT EXACTLY THRILLED TO HAVE HIM SLEEPING IN MY ROOM, EITHER... WE'RE STUFFED IN HERE LIKE SARDINES!

THE YAGAMI RESIDENCE

JUST LEAVE HER BE! SHE'S NOT OUR DAUGHTER ANY MORE!
HONEY, LET ME GO AND TRY TO PERSUADE HER TO COME BACK, ALL RIGHT?

BUT DEAR, YOU KNOW THAT IBUKI GETS SO STUBBORN ABOUT THINGS, JUST LIKE YOU.
THERE'S A REAL CHANCE THAT IF WE LEAVE HER ALONE, SHE MAY REALLY ELOPE WITH HIM!
WHAT?! WITH THAT DEPRESSING, SPINELESS, JOBLESS--
HONESTLY! HE SEEMED LIKE A PERFECTLY FINE PERSON TO ME!
RRIIP
IN ANY CASE, I HAVE A FEW THOUGHTS OF MY OWN.
SO YOU JUST RELAX AND GO TO WORK, DEAR.
......

HEY!? YAGAMI ?
I THOUGHT YOU WERE OUT WITH THE FLU ?!
SHHH! IT'S A SECRET-- DON'T TELL THE TEACHERS!

YOU'RE STAYING AT MR. GODAI'S? NO WAY!
YEP.
I HAD A HUGE FIGHT WITH MY DAD, AND... TAA-DAA.

I DON'T CARE IF I DO GET DISOWNED BECAUSE OF THIS!
I--I'M GOING TO LEAVE MY PAST AND MY PARENTS BEHIND AND JUST LIVE FOR LOVE!

AND SO...IT'S KINDA HARD FOR ME TO ADMIT THIS, BUT... JUST FOR...
UHH... TEMPORARY PURPOSES...
WELL, TO BE BLUNT...

GIVE ME MONEY !!
DOUGH! CASHOLA! LOOT!
YOU BETTER NOT DECLARE BANKRUPTCY AND DISAPPEAR!
YEAH! THIS IS A LOAN, YAGAMI !

Barber
CLOCK HILL BOOKS
VIDEO RENTAL
ODDS GROCER
CLOCK HILL
BAKERY

MRS. OTONASHI !
YAGAMI... ?
CLOCK HILL STATION
BAKER

I THOUGHT YOU WERE LOCKED UP IN ROOM FIVE?!
YEAH, WELL...
I HAD A LOT OF ERRANDS TO TAKE CARE OF, SO...

UMM, ACTUALLY... CAN YOU PLEASE COME SHOPPING WITH ME?
I REALLY DON'T KNOW THIS AREA AT ALL, SO PLEASE...?
......

A-1 SUPERMARKET

HOUSEWARES
KITCHEN
BATH
RICE
BAKERY

FWIP
LEMO HAIR
LEM HAI
LEM HAI

SHIM

OH, YEAH... MR. GODAI'S SLIPPERS LOOKED KINDA BEATEN UP. I THINK I'LL GET MATCHING PAIRS FOR US!

MAIDO
2F CAFE MAIDO
1F TURNIP
B1 RENTAL VIDEO
COFFEE & TEA

UNDIES & MORE
Lacey's
PERMARKET
CLOCK HILL BRANCH

IT'S MY TREAT, SINCE YOU HELPED ME OUT.
PLEASE, FEEL FREE TO ORDER WHATEVER YOU WANT.
LOOK... YAGAMI...

ARE YOU PLANNING TO MOVE INTO MAISON IKKOKU?

YAGAMI!!
UMM, WHAT'S YOUR CHEAPEST COFFEE?
THE HOUSE BLEND.
TWO OF THOSE, PLEASE.

YOU'RE RIGHT.
SURELY YOU REALIZE THAT NONE OF THIS IS GOING TO HELP MR. GODAI GET A JOB!
YAGAMI-- GO HOME !

I'VE BEEN A FOOL.
IT'S PROBABLY IMPOSSIBLE FOR EVEN MY FATHER TO GET MR. GODAI INTO MITSUTOMO WHEN THE INTERVIEW PERIOD IS CLOSED.

"YOU'RE RIGHT"... ? YOU MEAN YOU--

WH-WHAT MAKES YOU SAY THAT?!
'CAUSE IF MR. GODAI CAN'T FIND A JOB, HE'LL NEED MONEY FOR RENT AND STUFF, RIGHT?

I...
I WONDER IF I SHOULD QUIT SCHOOL...?

.....
.....

THEN YOU MEAN...
...YOU'LL BE GOING--

AND IT'S ALL MY FAULT, SO I'LL JUST HAVE TO GO TO WORK IN ORDER TO TAKE CARE OF HIM!
GREAT IDEA, HUH?!
MY HEAD HURTS...
LOOK... GETTING BACK TO REALITY, YAGAMI...
OH, I'M DEAD SERIOUS, MA'AM!
ARE YOU PLANNING TO ROPE HIM INTO SOMETHING HERE?
"ROPE HIM INTO..." ?
OH, NO-- I JUST WANT TO HELP OUT THE MAN I LOVE!
.....
.....
"THE MAN I LOVE," SHE SAYS!
THAT LITTLE... OOH!

MRS. OTONASHI... PLEASE DON'T MENTION THE CONVERSATION WE JUST HAD TO MR. GODAI, PLEASE?
I DON'T WANT TO STARTLE HIM.
NOT A CHANCE, KID!
HE'D DIE OF SHOCK!

BOWF!
OH...
OH!

MOM?!
IBUKI?

IBUKI, PLEASE DON'T!
I WANT TO DISCUSS THIS RATIONALLY! PLEASE--?

"RATION-ALLY"...?

IT'S OKAY-- PLEASE COME BACK.
TRUST YOUR MOTHER, WILL YOU, DEAR?!

....

MR. G, HERE!
HUH?!
FWUD
SUPERMARK
HEY!
HEY!
WHSSSH
IBUKI!
MARKET

HAH! SHE'S PROBABLY ON DAD'S SIDE ANYWAY!
KCHAK
SLAM
YOUR MOTHER'S CRYING OUT HERE!
THD THD THD THD
PERMARK
I SAID WAIT-- HEY!!
DMDMDMDM
WHSSSH

....
.....
IT'S THE TRUTH!
I WAS JUST TALKING TO MR. GODAI...
...AND I THINK HE'S A REALLY WONDERFUL PERSON.
IBUKI, HONEY...
MOTHER IS ON YOUR SIDE, DEAR.
THAT'S A LIE!

YES, I DO.
REALLY?
YOU REALLY THINK SO?

??
WHAT IN THE WORLD ARE THEY TALKING ABOUT?
I'M NOT SURE...
...BUT I'VE GOT A BAD FEELING ABOUT THIS.

BUT YOU SEE, IBUKI...
I REALLY DON'T THINK RIGHT NOW IS THE BEST TIME.
YOU STILL HAVE SCHOOL, AND--

I'LL QUIT SCHOOL!
NO, NO, YOU HAVE TO AT LEAST GRADUATE FROM HIGH SCHOOL!

ONCE YOU GRADUATE, WE CAN TAKE ANOTHER LOOK AT THE MARRIAGE.
SO PLEASE, COME HOME FOR NOW.
WHA--?!
WAIT A SEC!!

WH-WHAT IN THE WORLD DO YOU THINK YOU'RE SAYING?!?
SSH!

DON'T WORRY--IF I SAY THIS, I CAN CONVINCE HER TO COME BACK HOME WITH ME.
IT'S A LONG TIME BEFORE GRADUATION... I'M SURE SHE'LL GET OVER THIS OBSESSION BY THEN.

MOM...? THANK YOU FOR UNDER-STANDING...
...MY FEEL-INGS.

I MEAN... DAD'S PROBABLY GOING TO ARRANGE THINGS SO THAT I WON'T BE ABLE TO SEE MR. GODAI ANY MORE... I JUST **KNOW** IT!

I'M SO SORRY TO HAVE CAUSED YOU SUCH TROUBLE.

I'LL THINK UP A DIFFERENT PLAN AND COME BACK SOON.

I HOPE SO.

"A DIF-FERENT PLAN," SHE SAYS. I'LL BET!
WELL, THEN-- SHE LEAVES ME NO CHOICE.

COME WITH ME, GODAI !
HUH ?

YAGAMI? YAGAMI !!
NOK NOK

IF YOU'RE NOT GOING TO LEAVE, THEN STARTING TONIGHT--
--I'M GOING TO LET GODAI STAY IN MY ROOM! ALL RIGHT?!
URK !

B-B-BUT, M-MANAGER, WHERE ARE YOU GOING TO SLEEP?
TO-GETHER WITH YOU, OF COURSE!

AFTER ALL, WHAT CHOICE DO WE HAVE ?
I MEAN, WITH YOUR ROOM TAKEN HOSTAGE LIKE THIS, RIGHT?
....

HAH! I'M NOT GOING TO FALL FOR SUCH AN OBVIOUS TRICK!

THAT OLD WIDOW DOESN'T HAVE THE GUTS TO DO IT, NO WAY!

IF SHE DOESN'T, THEN THAT'S TOO BAD FOR HER!
YOU THINK SHE'LL COME OUT NOW?

Y-YES, OF COURSE! AFTER ALL, YOU'RE JUST SLEEPING IN MY ROOM.
R-R-REALLY ?!? A-ARE YOU SURE ?!

I SAID I'D LET YOU STAY THE NIGHT, AND THAT'S JUST WHAT I'LL DO!
"TOO BAD FOR HER"... YOU MEAN...?

WHAT ?!? SHE REALLY HAS A SERIOUS CRUSH ON HIM-- ?!
WHAT KIND OF MOTHER ARE YOU, ANY-WAY? I--
BOSS

WHAT?! YOU DIDN'T CHANGE HER MIND?!
MITSUTOMO

I DON'T UNDERSTAND IT. WHAT IN THE WORLD DOES SHE SEE IN HIM...?!
I'VE HEARD ENOUGH OF THIS NONSENSE!!
KACHIIIIING

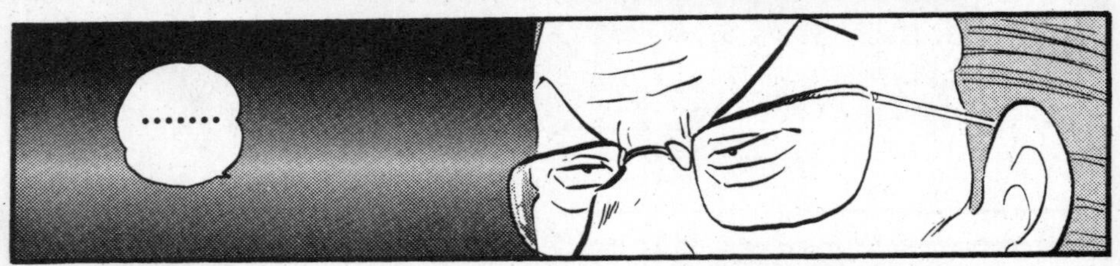
....

MAN... I CAN'T BELIEVE... SHE'S USUALLY SO STRAIT-LACED... WOW.
...IT'S STILL A BIG STEP, A BIG DEAL... FOR HER.
COFFEE

"I JUST WANT TO BE OF USE TO THE MAN I LOVE!"
BROTHER... SHE HAS NO IDEA WHAT THE REAL WORLD IS LIKE!
I'M NOT GOING TO JUST STAND ASIDE AND LET THAT... THAT CHILD DRAG HIM AROUND BY THE NOSE FOREVER!

"AFTER ALL, YOU'RE JUST SLEEPING IN MY ROOM."
EVEN THOUGH SHE SAID I'LL BE "JUST SLEEP-ING"...
PUBLIC BATHS

TO BEGIN WITH-- STRINGING ALONG AN ADULT MAN LIKE THAT--
--HOW CAN YOU CALL THAT LOVE?
RIGHT! FOR AS LONG AS SHE'S AROUND...
...I WON'T LET GODAI WITHIN TEN FEET OF ROOM FIVE AGAIN!

YOU KNOW... IF THE MANAGER IS WILLING TO LET ME STAY WITH HER, THEN MAYBE...
...JUST MAY-BE...

M-M-MANAGER, YOU MIND IF I...?
SHHHP
OF COURSE NOT! THAT'S WHY I LET YOU STAY WITH ME!

BUT... I FEAR I DO NOT YET EVEN HAVE A JOB TO SUPPORT US...
DON'T WORRY, MY DARLING! I'LL BE GLAD TO WORK TO FEED AND CLOTHE YOU!

OH, MY DEAREST DARLING--
FWUMP

......
KONNNGG
TAXI

AH, YOUNG GODAI-- JUST THE PERSON I WAS LOOKING FOR!
MR. Y-Y-YAGAMI ?

I WOULD LIKE YOU TO ACCOMPANY ME FOR A SHORT WHILE, IF YOU PLEASE.
SIR... ?

DON'T WORRY, SON. THERE'S JUST A FEW MORE THINGS I NEED TO KNOW ABOUT YOU, BEFORE... WELL, YOU KNOW.
EH?

WHOA! DON'T TELL ME HE'S REALLY GOING TO TRY TO GET ME INTO MITSU-TOMO...

WELL, UH, IN THAT CASE...
GIVE ME A MINUTE TO GO AND CHANGE, SIR.
OH, NO DON'T WORRY ABOUT IT.
I WAS JUST GOING TO HAVE YOU COME OVER TO OUR HOUSE.

THERE-- WITH THIS MUCH DISTANCE, AND THE TABLE BETWEEN OUR FUTONS...

IT'S NO BIG DEAL, SON. JUST THINK OF IT AS TWO OR THREE HOURS OF ORDINARY CONVERSATION. DON'T BE NERVOUS, ALL RIGHT?
SLAM
A-A-ALL RIGHT.
TAXI
BRRMMMB

...THERE SHOULDN'T BE ANY... INCIDENTS.
I HOPE.

DON'T TELL ME MR. GODAI...
...IS REALLY GONNA WALK WILLINGLY INTO THAT WIDOW'S LAIR?

EVEN IF HE WAS...
...HE'S NOT THE TYPE OF PERSON WHO WOULD... WOULD LET HER...

AND NOW, THE ELEVEN O'CLOCK NEWS...
EVENING NEWS
HE'S LATE.

WHAT'S WRONG WITH HIM THIS TIME?! HE PROMISED!!
HE'S MAKING ME LOOK STUPID!

D-DON'T TELL ME...
...HE'S WITH YAGAMI INSTEAD?!

KREEEE...

TP TP...

TM TM...
......
UMM... WHAT'S UP, MRS. OTONASHI?
OH, N-N-NOTHING. AND YOU...?
FWAP FWAP
HMM... MAYBE HE'S NOT HOME...
SHO... D'YOU LIKE KIDSH?
I WANT LOTSH OF GRAN'KIDSH FROM MY LI'L IBUKI, SHO YOU BETTER WANT KIDSH!
HIC
WAIT A SEC-- !!
WHAT IN THE WORLD ARE YOU GETTING AT HERE?!
OH, DEAR-- LOOK HOW LATE IT'S GOTTEN WITH YOU TWO CHATTERING ON!
YOU'LL JUST HAVE TO SPEND THE NIGHT, GODAI!

THE END OF JANUARY: FINAL EXAMS BEGIN.
YADDA YADDA
I'VE GOT IT WIRED, MAN!
ME TOO-- JUST TWO MORE CREDITS.
IT'S A SLAM-DUNK!
YADDA YADDA YADDA
BOY, YOU GOT THAT RIGHT-- *PARTY TIME!* EXAMS DONE, JOBS LINED UP...
SO HEY, WHEN WE'RE DONE WITH EXAMS WE OUGHTA... Y'KNOW...
HUH?
WHOA... SHHH!

PART 10
BEYOND LOVE AND HATE
YO!
YO, YOUR-SELF!
HOW ARE EXAMS COMING?
ALL RIGHT, I GUESS.
SHLUMP
DON'T FORGET, THE WORD "JOB" IS TABOO, RIGHT? GODAI HASN'T GOT...
YEAH, I KNOW, I KNOW! I FEEL SO BAD I CAN'T EVEN GET IN THE MOOD TO RANK HIM ABOUT IT.
PSST PSST PSST

HA HA HAA
HA HA HAA
......

GOOD, GOOD!
THAT'S GREAT!
...I'M STILL WAITING TO HEAR FROM TWO FIRMS, DAMN IT!!

RIIIING...
YES, FINAL EXAMS. HE--
NO, YUSAKU'S AT SCHOOL RIGHT NOW...
OH, HELLO, MRS. GODAI!
HELLO, MAISON IKKOKU...

LET ME PUT HIM ON THE LINE...
OH, HE JUST STEPPED IN THE DOOR!

...BECAUSE WE REALLY DON'T HAVE THE MONEY TO PUT YOU THROUGH ANOTHER YEAR OF SCHOOL, YUSAKU.
I'M PLEASED TO HEAR THAT...
OH, YEAH, I'LL PASS... SOMEHOW.
GRADU-ATION?

WELL, IN THE WORST-CASE SCENARIO, JUST COME HOME.
WE'LL LET YOU DELIVER TAKE-OUT ORDERS.
GEEZ, MOM! DON'T EVEN SAY THAT!!
I STILL HAVEN'T HEARD FROM TWO FIRMS!
PIYO
CHINGG
UMM... IS THERE SOME THING...?
YES... THIS ARRIVED FOR YOU.
IT'S FROM SOME COMPANY...
PIYO PIYO

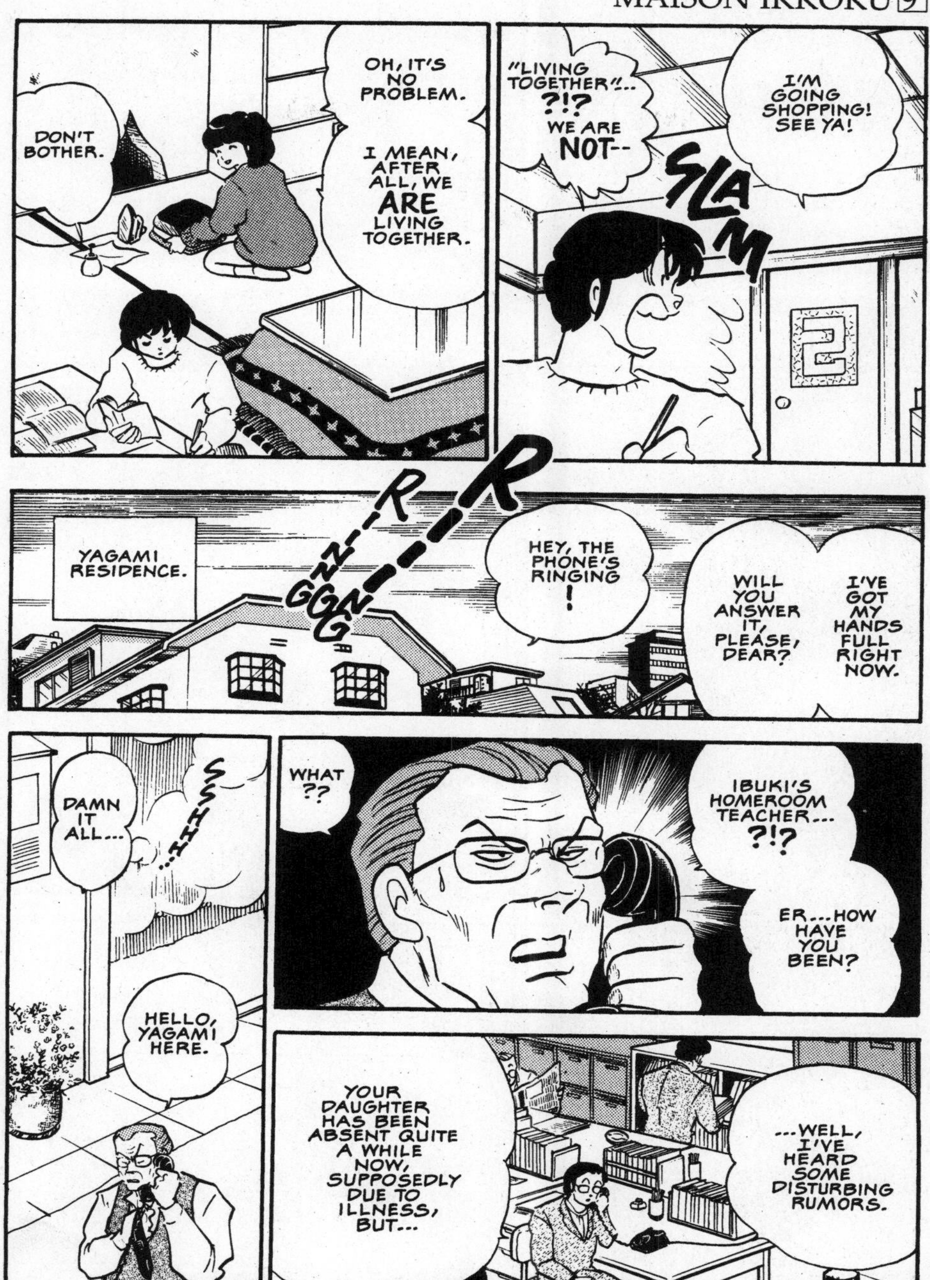
DON'T BOTHER.
OH, IT'S NO PROBLEM.
I MEAN, AFTER ALL, WE ARE LIVING TOGETHER.
"LIVING TOGETHER"!..?!? WE ARE NOT--
I'M GOING SHOPPING! SEE YA!
SLAM
YAGAMI RESIDENCE.
R-I-I-N-N-G-G-G
HEY, THE PHONE'S RINGING!
WILL YOU ANSWER IT, PLEASE, DEAR?
I'VE GOT MY HANDS FULL RIGHT NOW.
DAMN IT ALL...
SSHHH...
HELLO, YAGAMI HERE.
WHAT??
IBUKI'S HOMEROOM TEACHER...?!?
ER...HOW HAVE YOU BEEN?
...WELL, I'VE HEARD SOME DISTURBING RUMORS.
YOUR DAUGHTER HAS BEEN ABSENT QUITE A WHILE NOW, SUPPOSEDLY DUE TO ILLNESS, BUT...

I HEAR THAT IBUKI IS NOT SICK AT ALL...
...AND THAT, IN ACTUALITY, SHE HAS MOVED IN WITH A CERTAIN EX-STUDENT TEACHER.

....

SO... I WOULD LIKE TO CONFIRM THAT SHE HAS REALLY BEEN AT HOME, MR. YAGAMI.
WH-WHAT? I... SHE...
YES, OF COURSE!
KOFF KOFF

IT...IT'S JUST SUCH A TERRIBLE COLD, YOU SEE. I DON'T THINK SHE SHOULD EVEN TRY TALKING ON THE TELEPHONE.

?
ER... YOU SEE?
KOFF KOFF KOFF

DAMN IT! I CAN'T BELIEVE I ACTUALLY HAD TO LIE TO COVER FOR HER!
BAM
AND IT WON'T BE LONG BEFORE HER HOMEROOM TEACHER COMES BY TO PAY HER A VISIT.

WE'RE NOT GOING TO BE ABLE TO FOOL THEM FOREVER, YOU KNOW.
SO WHAT DO YOU EXPECT ME TO DO ABOUT IT?!

TO GET GODAI HIRED BY MITSUTOMO ENTERPRISES NOW...
...IS IMPOSSIBLE !
JUST PLAIN IMPOSSIBLE!!

WELL THEN... WHAT ABOUT ONE OF YOUR SUBSIDIARIES...?
....!!

......
......
SAY, MR. G-- ARE YOU COLD?
KLAK TAK TAK
HOW ABOUT A NICE CUP OF HOT COFFEE?
SPLSSSSH
OH, YEAH... THOSE GIRLIE MAGAZINES YOU HAD IN YOUR CLOSET?
I TOOK THEM IN TO THE USED BOOK STORE AND GOT US SOME CASH.
WHUD BAM
WHAT TIME DO YOUR EXAMS START TOMORROW, AGAIN?
FWHUMP
SKRITCH SKRATCH
BOY, YOU CAN'T AFFORD TO FAIL A SINGLE ONE, RIGHT?
OH, RATS! WE'RE ALMOST OUT OF SUGAR!

WILL YOU SHUT--
WHAM
HEY-HO, YUSAKU !!
OH, MAN-- THERE HE GOES, WASTING HIS TIME AGAIN.

WHAT FOR?
DON'T BOTHER HIM! HE'S TRYING TO STUDY!
C'MON, YOU GUYS!

I'VE STILL GOT ONE MORE COMPANY LEFT !!
SHE IS INDEED CORRECT. THEY WILL HIRE AGAIN NEXT YEAR.
IT WOULD BE EASIER IF HE JUST TOOK ANOTHER YEAR TO FINISH.

AS LONG AS I AM HERE, I AM NOT GOING TO LET ANYONE HOLD A PARTY IN THIS ROOM !!
WILL YOU PEOPLE PLEASE LEAVE HIM ALONE ?!?

TAKING IT RIGHT DOWN TO THE WIRE, HMM?
OH, YEAH? SEEMS TO ME YESTERDAY THERE WERE TWO LEFT!
LIFE LOOKS BETTER THROUGH THE BOTTOM OF A GLASS!
OOG!

HEY!
NO FAIR!
SLAM

THEY REALLY ARE A NOISY BUNCH, AREN'T THEY?
NO WONDER YOU NEVER GET ANY STUDYING DONE!
BUT I'LL PROTECT YOU, MR. G.

IF THERE IS ANYTHING I CAN DO...
...JUST SAY THE WORD!

......
....

OKAY, THEN.
CAN YOU JUST SIT THERE QUIETLY?

OH...?

JUST BE HERE WITH ME, AT MY SIDE.
THAT'S GOT TO BE WHAT HE MEANS!
YES, DEAR!

......
....

HEY !!
I CAN'T EXACTLY CONCENTRATE WITH YOU STARING AT ME LIKE THAT!

UMM... I'M S-S-SORRY.

NO, NO...
I DIDN'T MEAN... WELL, AS LONG AS YOU, UH... FORGET IT.

SSHHHHHHHH...

SIIIIGHHH
GAZING AT THE STRONG, BROAD SHOULDERS OF THE MAN I LOVE...
...I FEEL...

I...
I...
...
...

ZZZZZZ...

SHE'S CUTE WHEN SHE'S ASLEEP, ALL QUIET AND EVERY-THING, BUT...

IN ANY CASE... PEACE AT LAST.
I REALLY CAN'T AFFORD TO FAIL A SINGLE CLASS!

I HATE YOU, DADDY!!
GACK!
FWHAM FWHAM

I HATE YOU...
MMPH MMPH
TH-THAT LITTLE PAIN!
SHE'S A NUISANCE WHETHER SHE'S ASLEEP OR AWAKE...
BA-BUMP BA-BUMP BA-BUMP

I CAN'T TAKE THIS ANY MORE.
OKAY!
TOMORROW, I SETTLE THIS ONCE AND FOR ALL!

SHE'S RIGHT.
IF WE'RE TALKING ABOUT ONE OF MITSU-TOMO'S SMALLER SUBSIDI-ARIES, IT'S NOT ENTIRELY IMPOSSIBLE TO SQUEEZE HIM IN.

BUT...
...IF I SET THINGS UP AND GET HIM A JOB...
...THEN HE'LL BE ABLE TO...

PLEASE GIVE ME THE HAND OF YOUR DAUGHTER IN MARRIAGE!
NRRG!

I'M ON MY WAY, MANAGER!
OKAY... GOOD LUCK, GODAI!
PIYO PIY

UMM...WERE YOU ABLE TO STUDY ENOUGH?
YEAH, WELL...

LOOK, KYOKO-- NO MATTER WHAT, WHEN TODAY'S EXAMS ARE OVER, I'M GOING TO MEET WITH MR. YAGAMI...
...AND GET HIM TO TAKE BACK HIS DAUGHTER--!!
"GET HIM TO TAKE BACK HIS DAUGHTER"...?

MAYBE I'D BETTER COME ALONG...
NOPE! I CAN TAKE CARE OF IT!

I DON'T KNOW...
MR. YAGAMI'S A PRETTY TOUCHY, HOT-TEMPERED MAN. I REALLY WONDER IF GODAI WILL BE ABLE TO--
PIYO PIYO

MORNIN', MA'AM!
DID MR. GODAI LEAVE ALREADY?
YAWN...
WELL, SHE'S TAKING IT EASY!

TKD
INC
SECURITIES
BEEEEEEP
BEEEEEP
THE TIME AT THE TONE WILL BE TWELVE NOON, EXACTLY.

STOCKS BONDS
CAFE
MENU

"YOU HAVEN'T EVEN COME BY THESE LAST TWO OR THREE DAYS, NOT EVEN TO LECTURE HER.
WHERE'S YOUR 'MATURE, ADULT COMMON SENSE'?"
MUMBLE MUMBLE
LET'S SEE... "BESIDES, HOW CAN YOU CALL YOURSELF A FATHER?"

HELLO. SORRY TO KEEP YOU WAITING.

YEAH... MAY AS WELL BE TOUGH.
I GAVE UP ON GETTING INTO MITSUTOMO ENTERPRISES LONG AGO, SO THERE'S NO REASON FOR ME TO BE...
...ALL APOLOG-ETIC AND RESPECT-FUL AND LIKE THAT.

FINE, FINE.
I'M SORRY! PLEASE FORGIVE ME!
I, UH, I APOLOGIZE FOR TAKING UP YOUR VALUABLE TIME, SIR!
NO, NO, I'M SORRY, SIR!

SO...
CHIK

...WHAT IS THIS "BUSINESS" YOU WANTED TO DISCUSS?
FFFT

LOOK, "FATHER"...
......

I DON'T BELIEVE YOU HAVE THE RIGHT TO CALL ME "FATHER" JUST YET...
THAT'S NOT WHAT I...
WELL, OKAY THEN--MR. YAGAMI.

TO PUT IT BLUNTLY, I AM AT MY WITS' END.

THAT'S NOT SURPRISING. NO JOB, NO PROSPECTS, AND GRADUATION NOT FAR OFF...
THIS IS NOT ABOUT A JOB!!
STAB

LOOK, MR. YAGAMI--YOUR DAUGHTER'S NOT DOING ME ANY GOOD, AND I'D LIKE YOU TO TAKE HER BACK!
WHAT?!?
!!

HOW DARE YOU!

WHA--
!?
SO NOW SHE'S JUST A NUISANCE, EH?! WHY, YOU --
JUST BECAUSE YOU COULDN'T USE HER TO GET A JOB ?!?
BAM

HHHSSSHH

DAMN IT, I AM IN LOVE WITH MY LAND-LADY!
WHAM

....
....
...NOT EVEN NOW.
I NEVER HAD THE SLIGHTEST INTENTION TO "USE" YOUR DAUGHTER ...

SHE KNOWS.
SHE KNOWS, BUT SHE REFUSES TO BUDGE.
I MEAN, ABOUT YOU AND YOUR LAND-LADY...
DOES IBUKI KNOW?

GEEZ!
I SAY ONE THING AND HE TOTALLY GETS THE WRONG IDEA!
LADIES SHOES
SHOPPING
WHAT A CRANKY OLD FART!

IS THIS KASUMI, INC.?
THIS IS YAGAMI, FROM MITSUTOMO.
MITSUTOMO

...IS THERE ANY WAY YOU COULD SQUEEZE ONE MORE PERSON IN?
HE COMES WITH MY PERSONAL RECOMMENDATION, SO...
LOOK, I'M SORRY TO ASK YOU THIS SO LATE IN THE GAME, BUT...

THERE'S NO NEED FOR ME TO RELY ON MR. YAGAMI, ANYWAY.
KTAK KTAK
I'VE STILL GOT ONE MORE COMPANY LEFT!
IKKOKU
VIZ COMICS

BUT EVEN IF I GET INTO THAT ONE, I STILL HAVE TO...
...PASS ALL MY EXAMS AND GRADUATE.

ALL RIGHT, YOU GUYS--

GET OUT OF THIS ROOM!!

M-M-MANAGER...?!

KOFF

I HAVE HAD IT UP TO HERE WITH YOU PEOPLE!
SINCE YOU DON'T SEEM TO BE ABLE TO TAKE A HINT, LET ME GIVE IT TO YOU STRAIGHT-- IF YOU CONTINUE INTERFERING WITH AND DISRUPTING THE OTHER TENANTS' LIVES...
...I WILL EVICT YOU AND I AM NOT KIDDING!
YEAH, RIGHT. HAH!
WHO DO YA THINK YOU ARE, LADY? DIRTY HARRY OR SOMETHIN'?!
HIC
YAGAMI?!
YOU IDIOTS SERVED A HIGH SCHOOL STUDENT ALCOHOL?!
HMM?
I DIDN'T EVEN NOTICE HER!
MR. G...?
SLINK
DON' WORRY!
I'LL... I'LL WORK FOR THE BOTH OF USH...
AN' COOK AN' CLEAN AN' STUFF...
SO LET IT BE WRITTEN, SO LET IT BE DONE.
JUST RELAX AND TAKE ANOTHER YEAR OFF, KID!
NYA HAHA
YOU GUYS CAN MIND YOUR OWN DAMN BUSINESS!!

HELLO ?
HELLO ?

ANY-BODY HOME... ?

I TALKED TO YOUR FATHER, AND SETTLED THINGS WITH HIM.
YAGAMI, GO HOME.
WHOA !

THAT ISN'T FUNNY !!
"I'LL RETURN YOUR DAUGHTER TO YOU IN EXCHANGE FOR GETTING ME A JOB"..?
WHAT KIND OF DEAL DID YOU CUT?

LOOK-- EVEN I'VE GOT SOME PRIDE, YOU KNOW!
I DID NOTHING OF THE SORT!

ALL ALONG, I'VE BEEN MISUNDERSTOOD, HAD MY CHARACTER ASSASSINATED... AND NOW THIS!
WHY? WHY?!
Tp Tp

HEY, GODAI, SOME MAIL CAME FOR YOU TODAY.
I AM GOING TO GET A JOB ON MY OWN MERITS--

PIYO

IT APPEARS TO BE THE FINAL LETTER OF REJECTION.
SURE DOES.
LOOKS LIKE "DEATH BY HONORABLE DEFEAT," HUH?

ER... EXCUSE ME FOR INTERRUPTING, BUT...
M-MR. YAGAMI...?
DAD?!

YOUNG GODAI, I WANT YOU TO ACCEPT THIS LETTER OF INTRODUCTION AND I DON'T WANT TO HEAR ANY ARGUMENT.
IT WILL GUARANTEE YOU A JOB.
WHA--?

TAKE IT TO KASUMI, INC. IT'S A SMALL FIRM...
...ONE OF OUR MINOR SUBSIDIARIES... BUT I FIGURE YOU AREN'T EXACTLY IN A POSITION TO BE PICKY.

LOOK... I KNOW WE'VE BEEN THROUGH A LOT...
...BUT LET'S CALL IT A DRAW ON THIS.
B-B-BUT, SIR...

NOW, IBUKI... LET'S GO HOME.
HUH ?
B- BUT...
IF YOU DON'T GO HOME, I'M TAKING THE LETTER AND LEAVING... AND I WON'T BE BACK.
YOU MEAN... I HAVE TO GIVE UP...
BA-BUMP...
LADIES AND GENTLE-MEN, WE HAVE A DEAL!
MM-HM...
AND NOW--A TOAST TO CELEBRATE YOUNG GODAI FINALLY GETTING A JOB!!
YAHOOOOOOO!
I APOLOGIZE FOR THE TROUBLE MY DAUGHTER HAS CAUSED YOU, MRS. OTONASHI.
YEAH, SURE.
MR. G, DON'T FORGET YOU ONLY GOT THE JOB...
...BECAUSE I AGREED TO GIVE YOU UP-- FOR A LITTLE WHILE, ANYWAY!
WAIT A SEC... IS THIS REALLY THE WAY I WANT IT TO END...?!

PART 11

ROSE-COLORED GLASSES

HOME-STYLE
PUB
PUB
OPEN
ROOMS

JUST IN TIME!
HERE'S YOUR BEER.
YAMA YAMA
YADDA YADDA
YOUNG

OKAY, GUYS--
--WE ALL MANAGED TO GRADUATE AND GET A JOB, SO LET'S HEAR IT FOR US!!
CHEERS!!

TOO CLOSE FOR COMFORT, IN MY HUMBLE OPINION!
...YOU REALLY CUT IT CLOSE!
MAN, I GOTTA SAY, GODAI...

...HAVE REALLY BAD LUCK OR SOME-THING.
YOU KNOW, GODAI... YOU SEEM TO, I DUNNO...

COME ON, GUYS!
NO KIDDING... I SERIOUSLY THOUGHT YOU WEREN'T GONNA MAKE IT THIS TIME, KIDDO.

I'VE HAD A LIFETIME'S WORTH OF BAD LUCK IN THE LAST FEW YEARS.
I FIGURE I'VE USED IT ALL UP, SO FROM NOW IT'S CLEAR SAILING, HEY?

HEY, I NEVER HEARD WHERE YOU GOT IN!
KASUMI, INC.

"KASUMI, INC."? NEVER HEARD OF 'EM.
SAY...
...AREN'T THEY A COMPUTER SOFTWARE FIRM?

YEAH. THEY'RE PRETTY SMALL, BUT THEY'VE BEEN EXPANDING RAPIDLY THESE PAST COUPLE OF YEARS, SO...
COOL.

HA HA HA HA
I HEAR THAT WHEN COMPANIES GROW REALLY FAST THEY'RE NOT VERY STABLE, HUH?
THAT'S RIGHT!
TANKS.

KATAKK KATAK KATAK KATAK
PUB
Laser Image JAPAN

HMM... ALL THAT'S LEFT NOW IS GRADU-ATION.
THIS IS SO GREAT, NOT HAVING TO SWEAT ALL THE TIME!

NOW THAT I'VE GOTTEN A JOB, I'M NOT AN "UN-EMPLOYED LOSER" ANYMORE.

THE ONLY BIG THING I STILL HAVE TO DO IS THE PRO-POSAL.
I'VE GOTTA GET THE TIMING JUST RIGHT, I GUESS...

KYOKO, I HAVE JUST RECEIVED MY FIRST PAY-CHECK.
WILL YOU MARRY ME?
OF COURSE I WILL, YUSAKU! I'M SO GLAD I WAITED FOR YOU!

.....

I WONDER... HAS SHE REALLY JUST BEEN WAIT-ING...
...FOR ME TO GET A JOB?

I MEAN, LET'S THINK ABOUT IT--
--SHE KEEPS TURNING DOWN MITAKA'S PROPOSALS, AND HE'S GOT A REALLY GREAT JOB.

SO MAYBE I'VE GOT NOTHING TO LOSE BY PROPOSING A LITTLE EARLIER...
GEEZ, WHAT SHOULD I DO...?
HMM...

I'M HOME!
WEL-COME BACK!
PATA PATA
SORRY I'M SO LATE.
UM, GODAI...?
YES?

I GOT YOU A LITTLE SOMETHING... JUST TO CONGRATULATE YOU ON YOUR NEW JOB.
REALLY?
WOW, THANKS, KYOKO! REALLY!
I MEAN, YOU REALLY SHOULDN'T HAVE!
IT'S JUST A LITTLE THING.

HEY, A TIE--!!
JUST THE THING FOR A NEW "SALARY MAN," HMM?

JUST PUTTING IT ON MAKES ME FEEL LIKE I CAN'T FAIL!
I WOULDN'T COUNT ON IT.
HA HA HA
HO HO HO

....

OH, NO... I DIDN'T MEAN YOU'RE GOING TO FAIL... I...UM...
NO, I GET IT.

DON'T BE AFRAID TO EXPECT A LOT FROM ME, KYOKO.
I'M GOING TO WORK HARDER THAN EVER BEFORE IN MY LIFE.
WELL, I GUESS... BEING IN A SMALL FIRM...

YEAH. I SHOULD BE GIVEN MORE RESPONSIBILITY THAN IN A BIG ONE.
IT'LL BE EASIER TO SUCCEED, TO GET PRO-MOTED, IN A SMALLER COMPANY.

I'LL DO SOMETHING NICE FOR YOU WHEN I GET MY FIRST PAYCHECK.
OH, NO, NO! I'M SURE YOU'RE NOT GOING TO BE MAKING VERY MUCH...
SAKE
SAKE

ER... I MEAN...
....

SOMETHING TELLS ME SHE'S NOT EXPECTING MUCH OUTTA ME...

SO, I HEAR GODAI FINALLY GOT A JOB...
YES, HE DID.
I MUST SAY, I FIND EVEN MYSELF BREATHING A SIGH OF RELIEF.
GLINT TWINKLE GLEAM
AND SO... WHAT ARE YOU PLANNING TO DO, MY DEAR MS. OTONASHI?
"DO"...?
"WILL YOU MARRY ME, KYOKO?"
!!
.....
WELL...?
YOU KNOW IT'S ONLY A MATTER OF TIME UNTIL GODAI WILL BE SAYING THOSE WORDS, RIGHT?
HUH...?

GOOD HEAVENS, MITAKA !
YOU ALMOST GAVE ME A HEART ATTACK!
YOU DON'T LIKE THE IDEA?

N-NO, IT'S NOT THAT, BUT... WELL, YOU KNOW.
ANYWAY, STARTING A CAREER IS A MAJOR TURNING POINT IN ONE'S LIFE, YOU KNOW.

"I CAN'T AGREE TO MARRY HIM BECAUSE HE'S A PENNILESS STUDENT"...
THOSE SORTS OF EXCUSES DON'T WORK ANYMORE.
I...WHO, ME? I WASN'T...
LAVARRE

I HOPE YOU'LL BE ABLE TO MAKE UP YOUR MIND SOON, KYOKO.

YES...

THAT'S EASY FOR HIM TO SAY, BUT...
...LIFE ISN'T THAT SIMPLE, SO CUT-AND-DRIED!
KATAK KATAK
LOCK HILL
TATION

EVEN IF HE...
...DOES PROPOSE...

BE-SIDES...
HOME
CLOCK HILL MALL
SALON
DRUGS
JUST BECAUSE HE'S GOT A JOB...
...I DON'T THINK GODAI'S GOING TO MATURE INTO A RELIABLE AND DEPENDABLE MAN OVERNIGHT.

...IT'LL BE FOR AT LEAST ANOTHER TWO OR THREE YEARS.
...I DON'T THINK...

GEEZ, ISN'T THAT RUSHING THINGS A LITTLE BIT?
PRO-POSING AS SOON AS YOU GET YOUR FIRST PAYCHECK...?

ARE YOU PLANNING ON BOTH OF YOU WORKING?
YOU THINK SO?

I SUPPOSE NOT. NO SURPRISE, ANYWAY.
YOU DON'T HAVE ANY SAVINGS, DO YOU?
NOT TOO LIKELY, HUH?
WELL, I WAS HOPING TO HAVE HER QUIT BEING A LANDLADY, AND WE'D LIVE OFF OF MY EARNINGS ALONE, BUT...

I'M AMAZED BY YOUR PHENOMENAL ABILITY TO SEE THE DARK SIDE OF EVERY-THING.
I BET IT'LL BE TOUGH TO KEEP A ROOF OVER YOUR OWN HEAD, MUCH LESS ANOTHER PERSON, EH?

AND IT'S A SMALL FIRM, SO THE PAY WILL BE LOW.
YOU'RE NOT A STUDENT ANY MORE, SO YOUR FOLKS WILL PROBABLY STOP SENDING MONEY.
MEW MEW

WELL, MAYBE KYOKO...
OH, YEAH? SO WHERE DO YOU SEE ANY BRIGHT SIDE TO THIS?

HHSSSSSSSHH

...WOULDN'T MIND LIVING IN POVERTY !

EARTH TO GODAI !
SINCE WHEN HAVE YOU MET ANYBODY WHO LIKES LIVING IN POVERTY?
I'M NOT SAYING SHE'D LIKE IT.
IT'S JUST THAT SHE SEEMS LIKE THE FRUGAL TYPE, Y'KNOW?
SHE SEEMS TO BE GOOD AT MANAGING HOUSE-HOLD ACCOUNTS...
...SO WE COULD LIKE START OFF WITH A STUDIO OR SOME THING...

MY DARLING! I'M SO SORRY WE'RE POOR!
BUT DEAREST, I LOVE OUR COZY, SIMPLE LIFE!
BARGAIN
COUPON

HAVING A TINY APARTMENT MEANS I CAN ALWAYS BE NEAR YOU... LIKE THIS...
OH, KYOKO...

BROTHER, TALK ABOUT LOOKING AT THE WORLD THROUGH A ROSE-COLORED BRAIN.
...YOU'RE SUCH AN ANGEL!
NYAAA

MITSUTOMO
MITSUTOMO

MR. YAGAMI, I REALLY WONDER WHAT'S GOING ON THESE DAYS. TAKE SEKIGUCHI INDUSTRIES, FOR EXAMPLE...
SEKIGUCHI? OH, YOU MEAN--
--THOSE BANKRUPTCY RUMORS?

I HEAR THEY CAME VERY CLOSE TO DEFAULTING AGAIN LAST MONTH.
REALLY?

WAIT A SEC.

IS SOMETHING WRONG, MR. YAGAMI?
NO, NO, I'M FINE. IT'S JUST THAT WHAT YOU WERE SAYING REMINDED ME OF SOMETHING.

WHAT WAS IT...??
HMM... I CAN'T RECALL.

I GUESS IT COULDN'T HAVE BEEN VERY IMPORTANT THEN, RIGHT?
CARRY ON.
HA HA HA HAA...

PUBLIC BATH

OH, HI!
HEY, MANAGER !
COIN LAUNDRY

......
HUF HUF HUF
CAFE
COFFEE SHOP

I'M ON MY WAY HOME, TOO.
PERFECT TIMING, HUH?
PASSPORTS

OH, REALLY ?
...SOMEHOW IT STILL FEELS LIKE YOU'RE A STUDENT.
SEEING YOU LIKE THIS... I DON'T KNOW...

I GUESS I COME OFF AS BEING PRETTY IMMATURE, HUH?
I DIDN'T MEAN IT THAT WAY, GODAI.

WHEN I STARTED AS MANAGER, HE WAS STILL TRYING TO GET INTO COLLEGE.
IT'S SO STRANGE...

I...
...I'VE PRACTICALLY WATCHED HIM GROW UP.

I GUESS...
...IN SOME WAYS I THINK OF HIM MORE AS A LITTLE BROTHER THAN A POTENTIAL HUSBAND.

OH, YEAH-- I'M PLANNING TO LOOK FOR A NEW APARTMENT.

WHA-- ?

......

SO I THOUGHT I'D FIND AN APARTMENT THAT COMES WITH A BATHROOM...
I MEAN, I'VE GOT A JOB NOW, RIGHT?

I WANT TO SAY "DON'T GO!," BUT...
"...AND I WAS HOPING THAT YOU'D MOVE IN THERE WITH ME, TOO"... BUT I CAN'T QUITE SAY THAT YET.

ISN'T THAT RATHER... HEARTLESS?

W-WON'T IT BE PAINFUL FOR YOU TO LEAVE EVERYONE?
NOPE. NOT AT ALL.

YES, I DO.
YOU THINK SO?

...I CAN'T QUITE BRING MYSELF TO SAY IT.

WELL, THAT WAS CRUSHING.
WHAT'S SO BAD ABOUT THIS PLACE, ANYWAY?
I MEAN, I KNOW IT'S FULL OF FREAKS, AND THERE'S NO BATH OR SHOWER, AND THE TOILET'S SHARED, BUT STILL...!

I BET... IF HE LEAVES...
...HE WON'T THINK ABOUT ME ANY MORE.

OH, MRS. ICHINOSE.
WANT SOME COMPANY?

YOU WANT TO THROW A PARTY TO CELEBRATE HIS JOB...?
YEAH. WE HAVEN'T REALLY DONE ANYTHING OFFICIAL FOR HIM YET.

AND, TO COMBINE IT WITH A LITTLE HARASSMENT, WE THOUGHT WE'D MAKE IT AN ALL-NIGHT SESSION THE DAY BEFORE HIS GRADUATION CEREMONY... HEH HEH...
HONESTLY!

YOU KNOW, IT'S BECAUSE YOU ALL CONSTANTLY DO SUCH THINGS TO HIM...
...THAT HE'S PLANNING TO MOVE OUT!

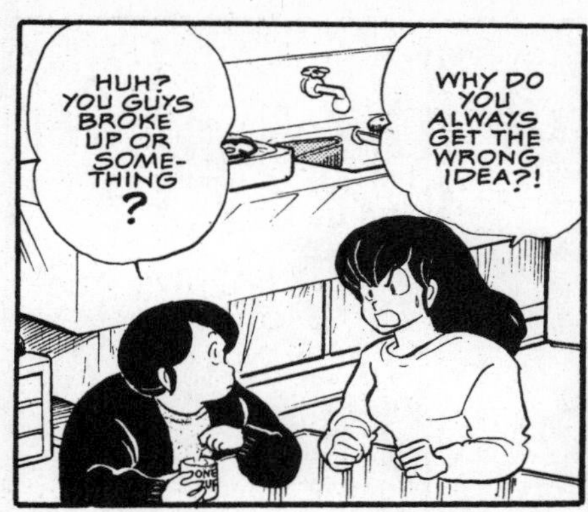
HUH? YOU GUYS BROKE UP OR SOME-THING ?
WHY DO YOU ALWAYS GET THE WRONG IDEA?!

COME ON! EVERYBODY KNOWS THE ONLY REASON HE STAYS HERE...
...IS BE-CAUSE OF YOU, KYOKO!
...
...

OH, PLEASE-- SPARE ME.
HE'S PROBABLY BEEN PLANNING ALL ALONG TO MOVE WHEN HE GOT A JOB.
I MEAN, IT IS A MAJOR TURNING POINT IN HIS LIFE.
SO WHY DID YOU TRY TO BLAME US FOR IT, THEN?

"EVERY-BODY KNOWS THE ONLY REASON...
...HE STAYS HERE IS BECAUSE OF YOU..."

REALLY !!
MEANING HE CHOSE AN APART-MENT WITH A BATH-ROOM... OVER ME!

AND SO, THE NIGHT BEFORE GRADU-ATION...
SO... WHERE'S OUR GUEST OF HONOR?
OH, RIGHT-- GODAI SAID...

...HE WAS GOING TO GO GET A TV FROM A FRIEND WHO'S MOVING BACK HOME.
A TV?
COME TO THINK OF IT, "WE" DON'T HAVE A TV, DO WE?
I'M SURROUNDED BY EXTREME POVERTY.
AND NOW HE'S PLANNING TO MOVE TO AN APARTMENT WITH A PRIVATE BATHROOM!
THE KID'S GOT SOME NERVE, HUH?
......
CHIPS

NO USE WAITING.
LET'S GET STARTED.
I AGREE.

"HERE'S TO BROTHER YOTSUYA, BROTHER YOTSUYA, BROTHER YOTSUYA!!"
WA HA HA HA HA HA
I'M HOME!
WE'VE BEEN WAITING FOR YOU!
CLAP CLAP CLAP
SO--THIS IS THE INFAMOUS FREE TV SET.
YOU'VE FINALLY GRADUATED, ALL RIGHT--YOU'VE BECOME A MASTER AT LIVING BY SCAVENGING OFF OF OTHERS.
SAY WHAT YOU LIKE, AKEMI.

WHAT CHOICE DOES HE HAVE?
IF HE'S GONNA TAKE THE MANAGER WITH HIM WHEN HE MOVES...
...HE'S GOT TO BE THRIFTY!
DAMN IT!!
DON'T SAY IT YET!
!

UH... SORRY ABOUT THAT.
SHE'S PRETTY DRUNK...
AH HAH!
SO THAT'S WHAT WAS GOING ON.

BWAHAHAHAHAHA
I'M STONE COLD SOBER, SONNY!
YEAH, RIGHT.
AND NEXT...

COMPUTER SOFTWARE DEVELOPER SEKIGUCHI INDUSTRIES, WHICH HAD BEEN GOING THROUGH A PERIOD OF EXPLOSIVE EXPANSION...
...HAS JUST DECLARED BANKRUPTCY, WITH DEBTS IN EXCESS OF...
BANKRUPTCY
NMN
TODAY'S TOP NEWS

WHOA... THINGS ARE REALLY TOUGH THESE DAYS, HUH?
COME ON, FOLKS, LET'S ALL TIE ONE ON, HUH...??
BLUP BLUP

ON THE SPRING IN THE YEAR OF MAISON IKKOKU, YUSAKU GODAI GRADUATES...

...AND IS IMMEDIATELY UN-EMPLOYED.

TO BE CONTINUED...

GET PULPED!

INTRODUCING A NEW LINE OF GRAPHIC NOVELS—THE HIPPEST MANGA FROM *PULP*, VIZ'S MONTHLY ANTHOLOGY

STRAIN, VOL. 1
GRAPHIC NOVEL

Assassin Mayo will *kill you* for *just $5*…

story by Buronson
art by Ryoichi Ikegami
b&w, 224 pages
$16.95 USA/$24.25 CAN

FROM THE AWARD-WINNING CREATOR OF SANCTUARY!

DANCE TILL TOMORROW, VOL. 1
GRAPHIC NOVEL

Suekichi is about to enroll in Love 101!

story & art by
Naoki Yamamoto
b&w, 216 pages
$15.95 USA/$21.50 CAN

"HIT THE BOOKS" WITH SEXY AYA!

BANANA FISH, VOL. 1
GRAPHIC NOVEL

The crime drama that revolutionized *shôjo* (girls') manga!

story & art by Akimi Yoshida • b&w, 192 pages
$15.95 USA/$21.50 CAN

"AN ADDICTION AND AN EMOTIONAL ROLLER-COASTER RIDE"—FREDERICK SCHODT, DREAMLAND JAPAN

Viz Comics • P.O. Box 77010 • San Francisco, CA 941
Phone: (415) 546-7073 • Fax: (415) 546-70
www.viz.com • www.j-pop.c